Praise for

Auschwitz

"A thoughtful overview of a place terrible to remember—and one that must always be remembered."　　—*Kirkus Reviews*

"Steinbacher . . . avoids extensive analysis or morality tales; the meaning of Auschwitz is in the details, which she provides with clinical precision."　　—*Publishers Weekly*

"This . . . poignant study is a worthy addition to any public or academic library, and is highly recommended."

—*Library Journal*

"Just 157 pages, Sybille Steinbacher's *Auschwitz: A History* is anything but slight. The German historian reveals details of the Polish city, starting from the thirteenth century, and then brings us to the horrors of the Nazi death camp—explaining why they chose that city to exterminate the Jews—the fate of the Germans who ran the place and its place in the postwar era."　　—*New York Post*

© Foto Seidel, Bochum

About the Author

SYBILLE STEINBACHER is an assistant professor in the faculty of modern and contemporary history at the Ruhr University, Bochum. During 2004–5 she was a visiting fellow for European studies at Harvard University. She has published a number of books on the history of concentration camps and their social context, including *"Musterstadt" Auschwitz: Germanisierungspolitik und Judenmord in Ostoberschlesien* (2000) and *Dachau: Die Stadt und das Konzentrationslager in der NS-Zeit* (1993). She lives in Germany.

Sybille Steinbacher

Auschwitz

A History

TRANSLATED BY SHAUN WHITESIDE

AN  BOOK

HARPER ⬤ PERENNIAL

NEW YORK ● LONDON ● TORONTO ● SYDNEY

HARPER ● PERENNIAL

Photograph on page 122 copyright © Państwowe Muzeum Auschwitz-Birkenau, Oświęcim.

First published in Germany under the title *Auschwitz: Geschichte und Nachgeschichte* by Verlag C. H. Beck in 2004.

This translation edition was first published in Great Britain by Penguin Books in 2005.

First U.S. hardcover edition of this book was published in 2005 by Ecco, an imprint of HarperCollins Publishers.

HarperCollins books may be purchased for educational, business, or sales promotional use. For information please write: Special Markets Department, HarperCollins Publishers, 10 East 53rd Street, New York, NY 10022.

First Harper Perennial edition published 2006.

Library of Congress Cataloging-in-Publication Data has been applied for.

ISBN-10: 0-06-082582-0 (pbk.)
ISBN-13: 978-0-06-082582-9 (pbk.)

06 07 08 09 10 ❖/RRD 10 9 8 7 6 5 4 3 2 1

Contents

Maps

Illustrations

Acknowledgments

The original idea for this book came from Norbert Frei, whom I should like to thank for the opportunity to write it as an addendum to our major research project about Auschwitz, completed in 2000. I should also like to thank him for our many conversations and his critical look through the manuscript. Gabriela Gworek supplied me with information on the post-war history of Auschwitz, and Ulrich Nolte and Simon Winder took care of the book on behalf of the publishers. I am also particularly grateful to the three of them. The book is dedicated to my grandmother Johanna Seidl and her brothers and sisters.

That was Auschwitz

She lies by the wall, groaning. The prisoners in the Sonderkommando, the special unit assigned to pull the corpses apart
and empty the gas chambers, find her: a sixteen-year-old
girl, covered with dead bodies. They carry her into an adjoin-
ing room and wrap her in a coat. No one has ever survived
gassing before. On his rounds, an SS Oberscharführer notices
the group. One of the prisoners pleads for the girl's life: once
she has regained her strength, please let her pass through the
gate and join the other women on the road-building unit. But
the guard shakes his head. The girl might talk. He beckons a
colleague over. He has no hesitation either. A bullet to the
back of the neck.

When the SS man yells at him, Stasio forgets to take off his
cap as camp regulations demand. With a blow to the head the
Scharführer hurls the young Pole to the ground and presses
the tip of his boot to his throat until blood flows from his
mouth. That evening Stasio's comrades carry his corpse back to
the camp on a stretcher. The Arbeitseinsatz (labour deployment
unit) must always stay complete. There are nineteen living
members and one dead one.

When Elisabeth is transferred to the prisoners' writing room,
her mother is still alive. Her siblings and her father are already
dead. She loses thirty relations in Auschwitz's gypsy camp,

including her aunt and her five sons and daughters, and another aunt, only two of whose ten children survive. Her mother doesn't survive either; she starves to death.

Numerous accounts and memoirs by prisoners in Auschwitz camp, like these brief summaries, have been passed down to us. They bear witness to the horror of events behind the barbed wire. The testimony of the victims is indispensable for any engagement with the subject of Auschwitz. It is only from their perspective that the scale of the crimes becomes properly apparent.

The subject

The history of Auschwitz is complex, and has not hitherto been the subject of a truly comprehensive work. This volume cannot fill that gap. Its aim is to represent the various aspects of the history of the Nazi concentration and extermination camp at Auschwitz in their most important contexts; to draw attention, within the wider perspective of political and social history, to the historical and political space in which the crimes were committed; and to sketch the subsequent history of the camp, including both the prosecution and punishment of the crimes after the end of the war, and the activities of Auschwitz deniers right up to the present day.

Auschwitz was the focus of the two main ideological ideas of the Nazi regime: it was the biggest stage for the mass murder of European Jewry, and at the same time a crystallization point of the policy of settlement and 'Germanization'. It was here that extermination and the conquest of *Lebensraum* ('living-space') merged in conceptual, temporal and spatial terms. As a concentration camp, an extermination camp and the hub of forced-labour deployment, Auschwitz embodies all aspects of the Nazi camp system. The connection between the intention to exterminate and industrial exploitation became an immediate reality here. The fact that the city of Auschwitz, influenced by centuries of Jewish tradition, became a 'German city' at the height of the genocide draws our attention to the area beyond the confines of the camp, and raises questions of the public perception of the crimes committed there.

I

The town of Auschwitz

Centuries as a border town

Germans first moved to the area around Oświęcim in the late thirteenth century. They began a settlement project whose 'completion' almost 700 years later became the impulse for and goal of the Nazis' brutal 'Germanization' policy'. Oświęcim, first mentioned in writing in 1178, lay on the dividing line between Slavs and Germans. Its name, derived from the old Polish *święty*, meaning 'saint', points towards the town's early adoption of Christianity.

Medieval colonization of the east arose out of the desire on the part of Poland's rulers to expand, to enhance Slavic culture through social, legal and economic systems, and thus bolster their power. The acceptance of German law – 'German' being less a national than a legal term – was a peaceful assimilation process that maintained, respected and promoted Slavic traditions. The settlers introduced German municipal law, because by medieval tradition legal systems were tied to people rather than to territories; they established the laws where they happened to live, and they did just that in Oświęcim around 1260.

The town at the confluence of the Vistula and the Soła soon became a small trade centre; it was the seat of the court and the capital of the duchy that bore its name. Oświęcim switched political allegiances many times over the centuries: in 1348 it was incorporated into the Holy Roman Empire, and German became its official language. But with the first medieval agrarian crisis, the German settler movement came to a stop in the middle of the fourteenth century, the Hussite wars brought the colonization of the east to a halt, and under Bohemian rule Czech became Oświęcim's official language. In 1457 the duchy – sold for 50,000 silver marks – came under the rule of the Polish crown, but temporarily maintained Silesian law before finally becoming a feudal possession of the Polish kings in 1565. When Prussia, Russia and Austria broke up the Polish state in 1772 and Austria annexed the areas between the Biała in the west and the Zbrucz in the east, including the great trading and cultural centres of Cracow and Lwów, the competing powers deployed their troops across the region, and in the same year Oświęcim passed into Austrian possession. German became the official language once more, the town bore the name Auschwitz, and it was in the new kingdom of Galicia and Lodomeria, within the Habsburg Empire. In the wake of a new revision of the boundaries – the second division of Poland in 1793 and the third in 1795 did not affect the town – Oświęcim entered the German Federation after the Vienna Congress in 1815, and remained part of it until the Federation broke up in 1866. The town supported the Habsburgs until the collapse of the monarchy in 1918, and the Emperor bore the title 'Duke of Auschwitz' until the very end.

Catholics and Jews

Attracted by the trade routes leading towards Lwów (Lemberg), Cracow, Wrocław (Breslau) and Zgorzelec (Görlitz), Jews first settled in Upper Silesia in the tenth and eleventh centuries. It may also have been at this time that they moved to Oświęcim, which lay at the crossroads of the main routes, but their presence is first recorded in 1457. Unlike the surrounding towns, Oświęcim had no law forbidding Jews to live and trade there. The Catholics did not unleash pogroms or carry out mass executions; they did not force the Jews to live in a ghetto, or drive them out of the city walls. During the first bloody wave of persecution in the modern era, the Chmielnitsky pogrom launched by the Cossacks in 1648–9, Jews were banished from the neighbouring towns, but in Oświęcim, perhaps because they were relatively few in number, they were left unmolested.

Unlike Prussia, which in the nineteenth century subjected the Polish inhabitants of the eastern provinces to unadulterated Prussian rule, Austria – under the pressure of political defeats abroad, and striving for reconciliation with Hungary – gave relatively free rein to the Galicians in their efforts to become Polish again and to achieve independent statehood. The Cisleithan crown territory of Galicia was awarded extensive rights of self-administration by the 1866 statute of autonomy. Poles took over the jobs of the Austrian officials, and the Polish language found its way back into the region's schools and administration. Oświęcim reacquired its original Polish name, and the street names became Polish as well.

With the economic revolutions that were taking place at the same time, the 'good Austrian era' began for Oświęcim's Jews. A number of decades followed in which the previously rather insignificant and poor Jewish community developed strongly in demographic and economic terms. The feudal and agrarian social order faded away, and with it went the old intermediary function of the east European Jews. Standing, as small shopkeepers, craftsmen, travelling salesmen, pub landlords and leaseholders, between the landed gentry, the peasantry and the state, they had been exposed to the corresponding social conflicts. This relationship, which had unfairly governed how Jews made a living and had for centuries denied them any economic advancement, disappeared. Jews were able to abandon their uncertain legal position, achieve complete equality as citizens, and exert considerable influence on culture and politics. A flourishing Jewish community emerged, and Auschwitz soon became an intellectual centre of orthodox Jews and also a site of significant Zionist associations. Even contemporaries spoke proudly of their own 'Oświęcim Jerusalem'.

While Galicia remained an agrarian country at the end of the nineteenth century, with almost 80 per cent of its inhabitants making their living through agriculture, and with a great deal of unemployment and poverty, Oświęcim developed into a prosperous town because of its proximity to the newly developed industrial belt of Upper Silesia and north-west Bohemia. The industrialization process gained pace when the town acquired a railway station in 1856. Thanks to its location between the coal-mining area around Katowice (Kattowitz)-Dombrowa and the industrial area of Bielsko (Bielitz), Oświęcim became a railway junction in 1900: three lines of the Emperor Ferdinand Northern Railway led directly to Cracow, Katowice and Vienna.

While Oświęcim's Catholics remained stuck in their agricultural jobs and rejected industrialization, only a small proportion of Jews continued working in their traditional trades. Most of them worked in the professions, particularly in the industrial sector. Many became big businessmen and opened banks and factories in Oświęcim and the surrounding area. Others even founded chemical factories and processing plants in the new industries. The oldest Jewish business was Jakob Haberfeld's distillery, founded in 1804, which made the town famous for many miles around with its trademark 'Schnapps from Oświęcim'.

Waves of immigration brought more Jews to Oświęcim than anyone else. By 1867 a total of 4,000 Jews had moved to the town, more than half the total of new incomers. Subsequently, the number of Jews came to exceed that of Catholic inhabitants. For a long time cooperation defined communal politics – although the Jews were expected to impose certain restrictions upon themselves. Only the post of deputy mayor was reserved for a Jew; the mayor was always a Catholic.

Before the Second World War the number of Germans

and people of German descent in Oświęcim was in-significant. In the multi-ethnic Austrian state, and in the non-homogeneous Polish national state, the subjective sense of belonging to an ethnic group was defined by the language one spoke. In the censuses held during the Habsburg period the inhabitants basically spoke only Polish. In 1880 only one resident gave German as his spoken language, in 1900 there were ten, and by the time of the 1921 census three inhabitants gave their ethnic identity as German. No real German minority group existed in Oświęcim, even though, in the census of December 1931, 3 per cent of the population declared German ethnicity. Nor did the town have German schools, German organizations, German churches, German associations or German newspapers. But three editorial offices in the town published Polish newspapers; there were also Jewish papers, some of them in Yiddish, including the journals of several Zionist groups.

The construction of a camp

During the powerful wave of emigration that had swept over Galicia from the end of the nineteenth century, Oświęcim, on the country's far western border, was the destination of thousands of new immigrants. They came to find work and a living as seasonal workers in nearby Prussia. They were known as *Sachsengänger*, literally 'people on their way to Saxony', a word derived from a Polish slang phrase used to mean 'going to work'.

The town's frontier location and the streams of

migrants led to the building of a special camp in Oświę-cim: the emigration camp for seasonal workers, with a national employment exchange. In October 1916 the town council sold the grounds, about three kilometres from the Old Town, to the Austrian government, and a year later the colony was adapted for emigrants and itinerant workers. But there were no barracks there, despite the fact that Oświęcim had served as a strategic base and military headquarters for the Austrian army in the First World War. The garrison was in Wadowice, about 15 kilometres away. The *Sachsengänger* camp consisted of twenty-two brick houses with hipped roofs, and ninety wooden barracks designed for 12,000 jobseekers. This was the barracks compound that the Nazis would transform into a concentration camp in 1940.

The *Sachsengänger* camp performed its function for about two years. After the First World War, when Oświęcim was part of the revived voivodeship of Cracow within the new Polish state, the employment exchange was quickly closed down, and the barracks passed into the hands of the state. It had various functions: part of it became a refugee centre for about 4,000 people fleeing Tešín (Teschener Land), the area between Oderberg and Bielsko, also known as Hultschiner Ländchen and the Olsa-Gebiet. Members of the Polish minority had fled from there after the area had been given to Czechoslovakia under the terms of the Versailles Treaty. In the former *Sachsengänger* camp the refugees set up a village with a school, an orchestra, a theatre, a sports association and a shooting club. A whole district came into being, called the New Town, or Oświęcim III (after the Old Town and the area around the railway station). Another part of the compound was rented by the state monopoly tobacco company, but most was requisitioned by the Polish army. One relic from the days of the *Sachsengänger* camp was the labour exchange, where a single office had survived in the barracks ground until the thirties.

In the wake of the border conflicts that broke out after the First World War, a referendum was held in March 1921, under the supervision of an inter-Allied government and plebiscite commission, concerning the territorial status of Upper Silesia. Oświęcim was not actually inside the area affected by the vote, but because of its proximity to the disputed territory the town was none the less involved in the border conflicts, because the neighbouring district of Pless was part of the plebiscite zone. During the three Silesian uprisings between 1919 and 1921 Oświęcim, which had been a centre of nationalistic and patriotic initiatives during the war, had become an outpost of armed Polish associations.

When the League of Nations Council, contrary to the results of the plebiscite, decided in October 1921 to divide Upper Silesia, giving two fifths of the land as well as the bulk of the industrial belt to Poland, the border crept further westwards. The part of Upper Silesia that had been Prussian and was now Polish was henceforth known in German as Ostoberschlesien – 'East Upper Silesia' – a description that established the continuing German claim to ownership of the region. As a frontier town in the far west of the Cracow voivodeship, until the Second World War Oświęcim remained highly significant as a Polish army garrison and the administrative centre of the district of the same name.

In the years leading up to the Second World War social misery and wretched economy conditions affected Oświęcim along with the whole of Poland. While this put a strain on the ability of Catholics and Jews to coexist, it did not destroy it. But Jews did begin to feel they were being held at arm's length. They were forbidden to use the bathing-place on the Soła, and access to the town park was closed to them. Jewish craftsmen received fewer commissions, and many of them were put out of work. Until the invasion of the Germans, however, the number of Jews in the town increased; at around 50 per cent of the population the rate was particularly high by the standards of western Galicia, which had a low Jewish population. Of the 14,000 or so people living in Oświęcim in September 1939 from 7,000 to over 8,000 – figures vary – were Jewish.

The start of war in 1939

The keystone of the Nazi policy of conquest was the acquisition of '*Lebensraum* in the East'. Adolf Hitler planned a new base of German power that would last for centuries, with a solidly German ethnic storehouse. As early as 1925, in *Mein Kampf*, he had announced the aggressive thrust of his *Lebensraum* policy, and claimed that the taking of 'the East' was nothing but the taking of a legitimate inheritance to which Germany had always been entitled.

In the spring of 1939 Hitler had still considered using Poland in an 'anti-Bolshevik campaign' against the Soviet Union, and incorporating it into a satellite system under German leadership. But when Poland refused to accept the role assigned to it, in April 1939 he terminated the non-aggression pact agreed five years previously. Poland went from being a potential ally to a disruptive factor in the German push for expansion. Hitler's policy became one of brutal aggression and unparalleled radicalism. Poland was conquered and politically destroyed, and was seen from that point onwards as a buffer zone against the Soviet Union.

With its measures of discrimination and extermination inspired by racial ideology, Nazi 'Germanization policy' differed fundamentally from the medieval settlement of the east. 'Germanization' was founded on anti-Slavism and eastwards-directed imperialism and involved the racial dogmas of *Weltanschauungspolitik* ('politics based on an overarching world view') centred around a nucleus of anti-Semitism. Its goal was the total destruction of the existing order. At the centre of the policy was the establishment of a German population, along with the expulsion and suppression of the native inhabitants. With the term 'Germanization', coined to legitimize east-wards-directed imperialist goals during the time of the Kaiser, the Third Reich made its central goal a restructuring of ethnicities leading to the victory of the 'Aryan race'. In the context of the Nazi 'new order of Europe', 'Germanization' meant a ruthless 'racial restructuring'. The plan was one of radical denationalization and the ruthless suppression of the native population.

When Hitler and Stalin, in their secret agreement of 23 August 1939, sealed the fourth division of Poland and the destruction of the country's independence, and drew up their zones of interest along the Narew, the Vistula and the San, half of all Polish territory, with a population of more than 20 million people, fell to the German Reich; 11.8 million inhabitants came under Soviet influence. By invading Poland, Germany came into possession of the country with the biggest Jewish population in Europe: roughly 3 million of the country's inhabitants, about 10 per cent of the overall Polish population, were Jews; around 1.7 million lived in the German and around 1.2 million in the Soviet sphere of interest.

Oświęcim, close to the border, was not far from Gliwice (Gleiwitz), where a unit of SS shock troops had, on the evening of 30 August 1939, stage-managed the *casus belli*. On the first day of the war the Luftwaffe attacked Oświęcim. The Germans were determined to take the strategically important railway station and the barracks of the 6th Polish Cavalry Battalion. The Polish soldiers moved out the same day, and transferred their base to Cracow, about 60 kilometres to the east. Many civilians also fled.

In the first days of September the bulk of those who left the town were Jews. By horse and cart and on foot, they travelled the poor roads towards Cracow, where most of them ended their trek in temporary lodgings. Some went on to Tarnów and Lwów, some headed for the Romanian, others for the Polish–Soviet, border. But after only a few days those who had stayed in Cracow took the road back home, for on 6 September the Wehrmacht invaded that city as well. Exhausted by their efforts, and hoping that things would be better at home, they retraced their steps.

Meanwhile the units of the 14th Army, under the orders of General Wilhelm List, had begun to advance. Behind the troops to the rear, the *Einsatzgruppe* ('action unit') *z.b.V.* (*zur besonderen Verwendung*: 'for special use') under SS-Obergruppenführer Udo von Woyrsch was marching towards Oświęcim. Himmler had hastily telegraphed through an order to form the unit on the evening of 3 September, because of heavy Polish resistance fighting in the industrial area of Upper Silesia. At Oświęcim a Polish regiment did try to break through the German lines, and managed to blow up the bridge over the Soła, the most important access route to the town. This meant that the German conquerors first had to lay a pontoon bridge over the river before they could take the town on 4 September 1939.

Only a week later the market square was called Adolf-Hitler-Platz, and the name of the town was Auschwitz. Although the streets, bridges and squares soon bore German names, for several weeks it was not even clear whether Auschwitz was part of the rapidly integrated region of East Upper Silesia, the still planned Reichsgau ('Reich administrative district') Beskidenland, or the General Government (the term applied by the Nazis to the rump Polish territory not actually annexed by the Reich), which had not yet been legally defined. Only on 26 October 1939, when the regulation concerning the establishment of the new border of the German Reich, drawn up by the Border Commission within the Reich

Ministry of the Interior, came into effect was the decision finally made: Auschwitz was part of Upper Silesia, and thus of the German Reich.

Hitler did not divide up the territory of Poland with a view to establishing German claims in the East once and for all. Rather he wanted to set in motion the 'Germanization' of the western Polish regions – East Upper Silesia, Danzig–West Prussia, Wartheland (generally known as the Warthegau) and East Prussia – as well as the economic exploitation of the rest of Poland as quickly as possible. In its efforts to establish a new territorial and economic order, the Border Commission accomplished its territorial task from the military, economic and transport points of view. The Reich gained over 90,000 square kilometres of land that had previously belonged to Poland, with four fifths of the country's industry and a population of about 10 million. Far more territory than had been claimed since the end of the First World War thus came to Germany.

The annexation of western Poland had an immediate effect on Auschwitz: the town was part of the German Reich – and did not, as is often suggested, lie in the geographically nebulous East. In other words: the largest extermination site in the Third Reich was (like Chelmno extermination camp in the Warthegau) on German soil – and it was also very near a town, and one that was shortly to be Germanized.

At the time of the annexation, however, there was hardly anyone in Auschwitz, which from now on belonged to the district of Bielitz (formerly Bielsko) in the newly formed government district of Kattowitz

MAP 1 *The location of Auschwitz in the German–Polish border zone*

(formerly Katowice), who could have been considered German in terms of Nazi racial ideas. This fact casts a sudden light on the scale of the racial task that the German civilian administration and the SS faced in Auschwitz. Given excessive historical importance because of the eastern settlers' movement in the Middle Ages, the brutal 'Germanization policy' became the ideological programme of the occupying forces everywhere in the annexed western Polish regions.

The western Polish territories were to be restructured as quickly as possible into a racially 'cleansed', ethnically homogeneous and, in alliance with fundamental measures designed to achieve an economic and social new order, economically viable region. This plan provided both for the construction of the German administration and the settlement of 'racially valuable Germans'. The goal was to expel all Jews and most Poles (meaning the non-Jewish native population), and strictly segregate them from the remaining Poles, Germans and people of German descent.

Early in October 1939 Hitler had given Heinrich Himmler, Reichsführer-SS and head of the German police, extensive additional powers in his new function as Reich Commissar for the Strengthening of German Nationhood to promote the establishment of Germans and people of German descent in the western Polish regions, while at the same time expelling the 'racially inferior' native population. In the wake of the first resettlement programme planned by Himmler, Auschwitz was to become the political, economic and cultural centre of Germans from the South Tyrol. But the plans were not definite, because after the defeat of France Himmler favoured Burgundy as the place to settle the South Tyroleans, followed by Lower Styria in Austria and the Crimea.

Meanwhile, in the region around Auschwitz it was becoming clear that 'Germanization' was not going to take place quite as easily as anticipated. The whole 'Eastern strip' of the government district of Kattowitz, of which Auschwitz was a part, proved to be hard to 'Germanize', because of its almost exclusively Polish and Jewish population. The settlement strategists agreed that the region was unsuitable as a base for Germans and people of German descent. Separated from the western districts of the government zone by the newly erected 'police border', a guarded rampart, from now on the 'Eastern strip' had second-class status in terms of territorial law. At least temporarily, this territory was exempt from 'Germanization'. For the native population of Auschwitz this was significant to the extent that it meant that they were – initially – safe from deportation.

Because of the situation in the 'Eastern strip' Auschwitz became a collecting-point for those Jews who had been deported from the western parts of Regierungs-bezirk ('government district') Kattowitz, where hurried 'Germanization' was under way; their numbers were constantly on the rise. The Jewish Elders' Council, set up on German orders, which was responsible for food and lodging, soon encountered quite insoluble problems. In the spring of 1940 Auschwitz had grown into one of the largest Jewish communities in the 'Eastern strip'. The Jews lived crammed together in the alleys of the

Old Town, isolated from the rest of the inhabitants and subjected to strict checks by German guards.

Among the Germans who now moved to Auschwitz were administrative officials, but also businessmen and *Treuhänder*, people who sold off expropriated Jewish and Polish companies. The move to the annexed Eastern regions gave inhabitants of the Old Reich (Germany in its 1937 borders), *Reichsdeutsche* ('Reich Germans') as they were called, ample opportunity to climb the social ladder. Corruption and unscrupulousness quickly became the pattern of behaviour among the conquerors. War euphoria, confidence in victory and a pioneering spirit turned into a lack of moral inhibition, and personal enrichment became the rule among the Germans in the East.

2

The concentration camp

Auschwitz in the National Socialist camp system

At the beginning of 1940 Auschwitz caught Himmler's eye. The Reichsführer-SS was in search of suitable areas all around the border regions to build concentration camps for political opponents. The former *Sachsengänger* camp was one of three possible locations that Erich von dem Bach-Zelewski had reported to Berlin from his SS-Oberabschnitt Süd-Ost ('SS Main District "South-East"'); other senior SS and police leaders came up with different suggestions. But the site in Auschwitz was by no means ideal as far as the SS experts were concerned: the buildings and barracks were dilapidated, the site was on swampy ground and afflicted by malaria, and ground-water resources were atrocious. Three commissions came to inspect the compound before the decision was reached in April 1940. For all its shortcomings, the concentration camp inspectors saw its benefits: the area had transport connections, it was at a railway junction, and it was easy to close off against the outside world. It is not certain, as has been suggested, that the crowded prisons in the Kattowitz government district prompted the final decision, and doubts surround Himmler's supposed order of 27 April 1940 that building should go ahead. It seems unlikely that the concentration camp inspectors would have taken an interest in regional problems, and after weeks of planning we may presume that an actual order was no longer necessary.

The first to suffer as a result of the camp's construction were about 1,200 unemployed Polish refugees from the Hultschiner Ländchen, who had lived next to the site and were now expelled, and Jews from Auschwitz, from whom the SS recruited about 300 men for the building work with the forced support of the Jewish Elders' Council. More than 500 large and small companies from the whole of the Reich were involved in the construction of and provision of equipment for the concentration camp: in civil engineering and construction work, and fittings and supplies of all kinds.

Auschwitz was the seventh concentration camp, after Dachau, Sachsenhausen, Buchenwald, Flossenbürg, Mauthausen and the women's camp in Ravensbrück. In other border areas, to the north-east as well as in the north, west and south-east, other camps were coming into being at the same time: as early as September 1939 the civilian prisoner camp in Stutthof near Danzig; in June 1940 Natzweiler concentration camp in Alsace; and in August 1940 Gross-Rosen concentration camp in the Old Reich area of Silesia, which was initially a sub-camp of Sachsenhausen and later became a camp in its own right.

At the top of the SS hierarchy in Auschwitz was Commandant Rudolf Höss, whom Himmler appointed

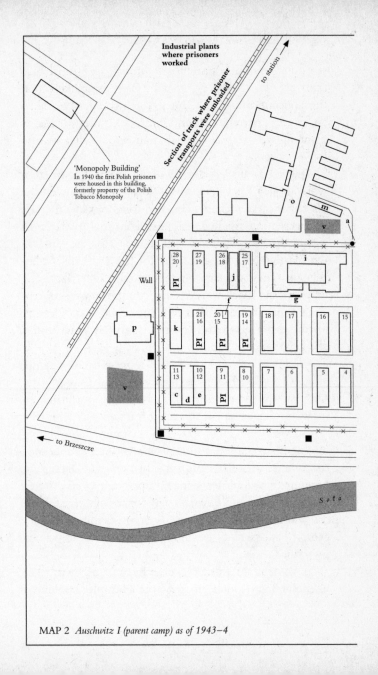

Industrial plants
where prisoners
worked

Section of track where prisoner
transports were unloaded

to station

'Monopoly Building'
In 1940 the first Polish prisoners
were housed in this building,
formerly property of the Polish
Tobacco Monopoly

Wall

MAP 2 *Auschwitz I (parent camp) as of 1943–4*

to Brzeszcze

Soła

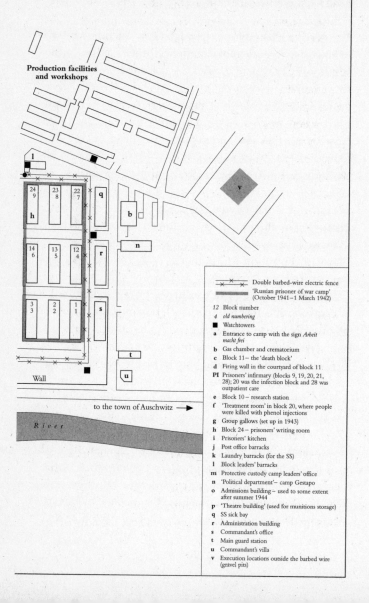

Production facilities and workshops

24 9	23 8	22 7
	h	

q

b

n

14 6	13 5	12 4

r

3 3	2 2	1 1

s

t

u

Wall

to the town of Auschwitz ➤

River

v

⠙⠽⠮⠿⠽⠿ Double barbed-wire electric fence

▬▬▬ 'Russian prisoner of war camp' (October 1941–1 March 1942)

12 Block number

4 *old numbering*

■ Watchtowers

a Entrance to camp with the sign *Arbeit macht frei*

b Gas chamber and crematorium

c Block 11 – the 'death block'

d Firing wall in the courtyard of block 11

PI Prisoners' infirmary (blocks 9, 19, 20, 21, 28); 20 was the infection block and 28 was outpatient care

e Block 10 – research station

f 'Treatment room' in block 20, where people were killed with phenol injections

g Group gallows (set up in 1943)

h Block 24 – prisoners' writing room

i Prisoners' kitchen

j Post office barracks

k Laundry barracks (for the SS)

l Block leaders' barracks

m Protective custody camp leaders' office

n 'Political department'– camp Gestapo

o Admissions building – used to some extent after summer 1944

p 'Theatre building' (used for munitions storage)

q SS sick bay

r Administration building

s Commandant's office

t Main guard station

u Commandant's villa

v Execution locations outside the barbed wire (gravel pits)

head of the new camp on 4 May 1940. As a *Blockführer* ('block leader') in Dachau and a *Schutzhaftlagerführer* ('protective custody camp leader') in Sachsenhausen, Höss had a great deal of experience of the camps. In the spring of 1940 he had headed the commission that came to Auschwitz to inspect the site. In all likelihood it was on his initiative that the slogan *Arbeit macht frei* ('Work makes you free') was placed above the camp gate of Auschwitz. The same inscription was prominently displayed at the camp entrances of Dachau and Sachsenhausen, and also in Flossenbürg and Ravensbrück. In *völkisch* ('ethnic German') and nationalist circles, the phrase had been circulating since the late nineteenth century. For the prisoners the motto was one of sheer cynicism, because work in the forced regime of the Nazi concentration camps meant exploitation, beatings, harassment and death.

As commandant, Höss was in charge of the SS guards, was responsible for the security of the camp, and handled all internal matters. The six departments that comprised the staff of the camp administration (every camp was organized identically, and this structure remained unchanged in all cases until the end of the war) were as follows: department I, the commandant's office, was run by the adjutant to the camp commandant, and was responsible for SS personnel management, correspondence and the arming of the troops. Department II was the political department, the representatives of the Gestapo and the Kripo ('Criminal Police') in the camp, who were subordinate to the local Gestapo or the Reichssicherheitshauptamt ('Reich Security Central Office'), or

RSHA, set up at the start of the war, and who were responsible for the interrogation of prisoners. Department III encompassed the running of 'protective custody'; the senior 'protective custody camp leader' covered for the commandant and was in charge of the SS *Kommandoführer* ('squad leaders'), *Arbeitsdienstführer* ('work duty leaders'), *Rapportführer* ('report leaders') and block leaders deployed in the camp. Department IV was administration; department V was the base doctor and the medical staff, department VI covered the training and welfare of the SS troops. The SS central building administration was part of the SS garrison, but was not incorporated into the camp administration any more than were the SS troop stores or the SS agricultural estate.

By the end of 1940 the camp building site in Auschwitz was so large that a decision had to be made in the first general building plan as to the location of the 'protective custody' camp, industrial site, workshops, barracks area, troop stores, SS housing and the agricultural estate. Zone after zone was added to the camp compound; the site was extended to such an extent that the SS soon acquired whole villages, forests, ponds and farmland: the so-called SS 'zone of interest', finally about 40 square kilometres in area. Surrounded by SS guards in the inner and outer cordons – the inner cordon ran round the camp grounds, the outer one around the SS zone of interest – the area was surrounded by warning signs, concrete walls, watchtowers and double-depth, electrified barbed-wire fences that were illuminated at night.

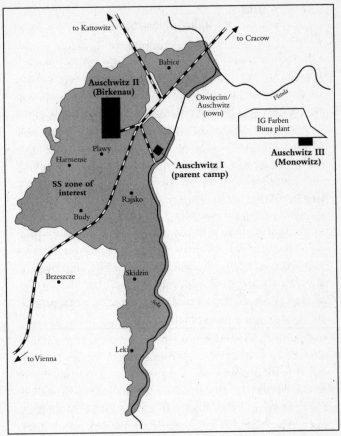

MAP 3 *The SS zone of interest, Auschwitz*

The prisoners

On 14 June 1940 Auschwitz went into operation as a quarantine or transit camp. Floods of prisoners were 'sorted' there, groups were broken up and reassembled, and after a certain period of quarantine transported to another camp. It soon became clear that Auschwitz was to be a permanent institution. The 728 Polish prisoners delivered to the camp on 'foundation day', most of them schoolchildren, students and soldiers, came from Tarnów prison near Cracow; a further 313 followed six days later from the Wiśnicz Nowy prison in the General Government. Major transports of 1,666 and 1,705 prisoners arrived from Warsaw in August and September of 1940. Almost all the prisoners were initially employed in the construction of the camp, which, because of the dilapidated state of the buildings and the lack of material, took much longer than planned.

At no other place in the Nazi sphere of power were so many people killed as in Auschwitz. But the camp was by no means the centre of the genocide of the European Jews from the very outset. Auschwitz was opened as a prison for Polish political prisoners. Within the Nazi camp system Auschwitz was at first one of many compulsory institutions for the isolation and 'disciplining' of opponents. The only unusual thing was its capacity to accommodate up to 10,000 prisoners (at the beginning of the war there were about 25,000 in all the other concentration camps put together), which had been worked out on the basis that the occupying forces in conquered Poland expected to arrest numerous political enemies.

During the initial phase, the majority of the inmates were not Jews; those affected by persecution and the arbitrary use of power tended rather to be members of former Polish political parties and organizations, members of the intelligentsia and anyone potentially involved in the Polish nationalist resistance, above all teachers, scientists, clerics and doctors. Until around the middle of 1942, during the 'Polish phase' of the camp's history, the number of Jews, most of whom were arrested for political reasons, remained relatively small. During this period the prisoners were not yet being systematically murdered, but died of hunger, harassment and intolerable working conditions; they were beaten, hanged and shot to death by the SS.

Their treatment, their everyday life and their response to acts of violence and cruelty are difficult to describe. It is relatively easy to outline the reception process, living conditions and first experiences of the camp, but what is hard to grasp is the constant pressure to conform to which the prisoners were exposed, because conditions in the camp changed often. And the individual suffering of a prisoner can barely be captured in words.

Once they had been handed over, the systematic humiliation began. Trucks brought the prisoners straight to the camp gate; smaller transports collected the SS from the station 2 kilometres away. Later, trains stopped at a spur where some loading ramps had been set up; one reached as far as the camp. Upon registration, each prisoner was given a number, which from that point onwards replaced his or her name. The prisoners had to undress, their heads and bodies were shaved, and they were beaten all the way to the showers. They changed their clothes for striped suits made of coarse canvas, a thin set for the summer, and a thicker, but barely warming one for the winter; they also received heavy wooden shoes. They had their photographs taken, in police style; but when they ran out of film the SS soon started photographing only Reich Germans.

A scrap of fabric with the prisoner's number was worn at chest height on the left of the jacket. Below it was a triangle, known as a *Winkel*, point downwards, the colour of which (standardized in all camps from 1937 to 1938) showed the prisoner's category, and it was also applied to the hem of the right trouser leg. A red triangle indicated that the reasons for imprisonment were political. Green *Winkel* were worn by 'criminals' and also by 'prisoners in preventive custody', known in the jargon of the camp as 'professional criminals'. The colour black stood for 'anti-social types', meaning prostitutes and also Sinti and Roma. The triangles of the Jehovah's Witnesses, known as *Bibelforscher* or 'Bible-researchers', were purple. Homosexuals wore pink *Winkel*, emigrants blue and Jews, who formed a category of their own regardless of nationality, yellow. A letter on the triangle gave the nationality of non-Jews: 'P', for example, meant Pole; Reich Germans – most of them falling under the category of 'criminals' – were not obliged to wear a letter. Jews had to wear a different-coloured *Winkel* over the yellow one according to the reason for their imprisonment, so that their clothes were adorned with a kind of star of

David; from mid-1944 a yellow strip over the *Winkel* replaced the second triangle.

The prisoners' hierarchy ran along racial lines: only Reich Germans were assessed as *Bevorzugte Häftlinge* ('preferred prisoners'), a category that granted all kinds of privileges. Those who were *bevorzugt*, or *BV*, and who were among the so-called camp elite, were permitted to go for a walk outside the camp grounds under SS supervision and wear civilian clothes, grow their hair and wear a wristwatch. After the Reich Germans came the non-Jewish prisoners of other nationalities. Their positions rose with the duration of their imprisonment: the longer prisoners had survived in the camp (identifiable by their low prisoner number), the better was their position, even where the SS were concerned. At the bottom came Jews, who were refused positions within the camp hierarchy until 1943–4, by which time hardly any 'Aryan' camp inmates were being delivered.

Erziehungshäftlinge ('re-education prisoners'), who were sent to Auschwitz from mid-July 1941 and placed in special blocks redesigned as labour re-education camps, were identified by a large 'E' rather than a *Winkel*. Most of the prisoners falling under this category, chiefly on grounds of a 'lack of labour morale', were Poles from the Kattowitz government district. Labour re-education prisoners, of which there were about 12,000 in Auschwitz, including 2,000 women, came under the auspices of the Gestapo throughout the Reich, and were for that reason assigned to the political department in the camp. Their sentences were officially limited to between forty-two and fifty-six days, but in fact often lasted from three to six months. Prisoners who had been released went home and were vowed to silence. But many did not survive their imprisonment.

The 'quarantine period', as it was called, that immediately followed the delivery process for all prisoners meant isolation, harassment and murderous drills. Anyone too weak to endure humiliating insults while standing to attention or exercising for hours at a time was punished by the SS, with blows, buckets of ice-cold water and hard work. Weak and humiliated, many took refuge in suicide. But those who managed to survive the first few weeks clung to the hope that things might get better in the work units. They were to be sorely disappointed, because these units had to do at least ten hours' forced labour every day, first in the construction of the camp, and later for German industrial companies.

After being woken – in summer at half-past four, in winter an hour later – the prisoners were herded to the washrooms, and then hurried to morning roll-call. Often the work units left the camp to the sound of the prisoners' orchestra, which was forced to play. The construction site, the gravel pit and the timber yard were particularly feared as units that hardly anyone survived. In the evening the roll-call could sometimes last for hours, particularly if there had been deaths during the day; in such cases lights-out, scheduled for nine o'clock, did not come until long after midnight.

'Offences' such as a missing button, an unsuitable facial expression or a sloppily washed food bowl were subject to many different penalties: punishment by beating, fatigues, detention. Strict detention meant solitary imprisonment with bread and water; prisoners might also be kept in darkness or in cells where they could only stand, or they were hung from posts with arms raised high and tied behind their back. One of the worst penalties, applied for example in cases of attempted escape, was the punishment unit, because hardly anyone survived the digging and building work. Prisoners in the punishment units were specially marked: apart from the coloured *Winkel*, they wore a black dot on their clothes; those suspected of planning an escape had to wear a red dot and the letters *iL*, for *im Lager* ('in the camp').

On Sundays, when no work was done, the prisoners were allowed to write to their families. For one Reichsmark they had to buy a preprinted sheet of writing paper and stamps in the camp canteen. They were able to receive small amounts of money (and later also food parcels) from their relatives. But anyone without money had to trade bread for paper and stamps. Anyone who needed the help of a fellow prisoner to write in German, the required language, had to pay with their bread ration as well. The SS censored the letters, cutting out unacceptable passages or making them illegible in some other way. One sentence was always to be included: 'I am healthy, I am fine.'

The prisoners lived in wretched conditions. They slept tightly crammed together, initially on sacks filled with straw, on the floor. Several thousand shared two wells for washing, and a single latrine trench. Sanitary equipment was not installed until February 1941: there was one latrine room per prisoner block, and one room with a channel for washing in. After wooden bed-frames had been set up, six prisoners and more had to share a bunk-bed designed for three. In the morning there was unsweetened coffee substitute or herbal tea, and at lunchtime watery soup with no meat, but with parsnips, potatoes or millet, and at dinnertime bread which was usually old and dry and often mouldy, and which had to do for breakfast the following morning as well. Weakness, exhaustion and illness were the consequences of malnutrition. Those who were reduced to skin and bone and barely capable of life, and had to resort to eating leftovers, potato peel and rotten turnips, were known in prison slang as *Muselmänner* ('Moslems') and avoided.

Neither in Auschwitz nor anywhere else did the camp inmates form a homogeneous 'community of prisoners'; they differed too greatly in terms of national origin, and of social, political and religious affiliations. Because of the many kinds of pressure they had to endure, because they were in the hands of the SS, and because there was so little room for manoeuvre, the prisoners were often in competition with one another. Their everyday life was informed by strenuous attempts to cope in the camp, and unwritten laws governed the internal power structures.

The so-called prisoners' self-administration, an SS system of patronage defined by the arbitrary use of power, further stirred up conflicts between the prisoners. In their positions as the most senior prisoners in the camp or the blocks, as *Stubendienste* ('barrack-room orderlies'), *Blockschreiber* ('block clerks'), *Kapos* ('overseers') and *Kommandierte* ('trusties'), the prisoners who acted as *Funktionshäftlinge* ('functionary prisoners'), and who were mostly 'Aryan', formed the so-called *Lager-prominenz* – the camp elite. It was their task to keep watch over fellow prisoners and, in the interests of the SS, to ensure the smooth day-to-day running of the camp. Only a very few prisoners tried to use their positions to the benefit of their fellow prisoners. The 'functionaries' enjoyed privileges, were barely threatened with violence and harassment, and had better accommodation and food than anyone else. An SS-controlled camp hierarchy came into being; in Auschwitz it remained for a long time in the hands of mostly Reich German prisoners, who had been detained as 'prisoners in preventive custody', and who occupied the coveted 'functionary' posts even in the early days of the camp.

On 6 July 1940 Tadeusz Wiejowski from Tarnów was the first prisoner to succeed in escaping. He managed to get out by a side exit from the camp, ran towards the station, climbed aboard a freight train and fled. The Polish population in the surrounding area were immediately suspected of helping a fugitive, because the Polish civilian workers of one of the construction companies had given aid to Wiejowski. So for weeks the locals were subjected to reprisals. Houses were torn down and their inhabitants transported to the Old Reich to form forced-labour units.

Civilian workers were the most important connection between the prisoners and the outside world; at times there were more than 1,000 of them based in the camp, employed as bricklayers, fitters, bulldozer drivers and foremen. They were identified by special papers, green armbands bearing the name of their company and a staff number. It was through their help that letters left the camp, and thanks to them that many prisoners managed to escape. Two thirds of all attempted escapes took place during the major expansion of the camp between 1943 and 1944. More prisoners escaped from Auschwitz than from almost any other camp. Half of those who attempted an escape were Poles. Of a total of 802 escapees of all nations (757 men and 45 women), 144 are known to have got away; most of the others (at least 327) were picked up, and many were shot.

Whenever a prisoner had escaped, the whole camp had to appear for a punitive roll-call, and the police force in the Kattowitz district took up the search, using all its resources, including motorized SS units and men with trained tracking dogs. SS guards then set up posts surrounding the camp grounds at a distance of a few hundred metres, and the outer cordon remained in position even during the night. If a prisoner was caught after a break-out, he could expect to be executed. But each time this happened the price was also paid by ten to twelve prisoners from the escapee's work unit, whom the SS either placed in a punishment unit to intimidate the others or simply shot. Polish civilians caught helping escapees were immediately sent to the camp; if they could not be found, the SS arrested their families.

Despite the severe punishments, the inmates of the camp could expect help from the Polish population. Prisoners who were employed on survey work, road-building, river management, demolition and in the carpenter's yard of the Salesian monastery in the town of

Auschwitz managed to establish contacts. Bread, medication, money, clothes and newspapers were given to the prisoners by local civilians, the smuggling of secret messages and letters flourished, and reports of the crimes being perpetrated in the camp circulated.

In Auschwitz, Brzeczsze and other towns in the surrounding area these relief efforts developed into an organized network, formed chiefly of political resistance groups and considerably influenced by the Catholic parish of the Assumption of the Virgin Mary in the town of Auschwitz. These actions on behalf of the prisoners were a manifestation of massive resistance against the occupying regime. With the concentration camp – the instrument of their oppression – right before their eyes, hundreds of people took part in a patriotic campaign – often at great risk to themselves. Help was at first offered by individuals, and then also by whole families and groups that rapidly formed, including the Armed Struggle Association (later the Armia Krajowa), the Peasants' Party, the Polish Socialist Party, conservative peasant battalions, a peasant liberation organization, the Communist Polish Workers' Party, the scouting community and the local unit of the People's Army.

These actions were astonishing, given the difficult conditions that prevailed, because unlike in the General Government the rigorous 'Germanization policy' in the annexed Eastern regions meant that the structures of the Polish administration had not been preserved; Polish staff were not tolerated even in lowly official positions. Against this background the activities of the resistance groups in Auschwitz are all the more significant. Although the organizations had no opportunity to use armed force until the end of the war, their struggle was important because it showed that the population would not allow itself to be obliterated even in an area where the occupying forces employed extreme measures of control and punishment.

Despite the SS terror, organized resistance also developed within the camp, sustained at first by socialist and nationalist inmates who formed into a unified organization early in 1942. With the number of prisoners dispatched there, the in-camp resistance movement fragmented into various national and religious groups, most of them led by socialists and communists. French, Yugoslavian, Austrian, Russian, Czech and Jewish prisoners all formed their own conspiratorial circles within the growing camp conglomerate of Auschwitz, at first acting independently, but soon seeking to cooperate with one another. Under a common leadership, 'Combat Group Auschwitz' arose, decisively held together by Hermann Langbein, a veteran of the Spanish Civil War from Vienna, who had been deported to Auschwitz in August 1942. Cells, groups and sections arose, and the members of the resistance group gradually came to occupy posts in the prisoner hierarchy, including positions in the commandant's office and the political department, the prisoners' writing room, the *Arbeitseinsatz* ('labour deployment') office and the prisoners' sick bay. Many forms of self-help were developed, food and papers were acquired, escape attempts organized, acts of sabotage initiated. Contact was made with the outside world. SS documents or copies of them got out and documented the crimes being committed in the camp.

The conspirators had had as their goal an armed uprising since the spring of 1942. But the Polish underground movement warned against such an action, because given the German position of power support from the Allies was barely conceivable. So a jointly organized revolt never occurred, but spontaneous rebellions prompted by the immediate threat of death, and *ad hoc* attempts at uprisings, did take place. Although these revolts were brutally suppressed, they did demonstrate the will of the prisoners not to take the crimes of the Lager-SS (Camp SS) sitting down.

The Lager-SS

The first camp guards came from an SS cavalry unit based in Cracow, but soon trained troops from Buchenwald and other camps served in Auschwitz. The SS men were at first housed in barracks and schools, but gradually houses and whole streets in the town were commandeered for them. If the SS guard units still numbered around 700 people in March 1941, by June 1942 there were three times that number. In August 1944, after the evacuation of the camp had begun, more than 3,300 were serving in Auschwitz. The peak of almost 4,500 SS men was reached in January 1945 during the final phase of the evacuation. By the end of the war a total of about 7,000 people attached to the SS had been working in the camp, including – as guards, SS messenger girls and medically trained SS nurses – some 200 women. Unlike men, women were not allowed to wear SS rank insignia, received no battle decorations and were employees rather than members of the SS. A great variety in terms of age, level of education and origin was just as characteristic of the camp staff as were changes in personnel. In the five years of the camp's existence, the members of the guard units were changed about twice on average.

The SS settlement in Auschwitz soon expanded into a district of its own. Life in the new quarter was supplied with many modern comforts. There were a coffee house, a swimming-pool, a library, kindergartens, schools, and medical and dental practices. The medical care provided by the camp department doctor was highly valued by the SS forces and their families. SS doctors ran a hospital with in-patient facilities, 'family doctors' held 'family consultations'. Many fiancées and wives with children followed their husbands to Auschwitz. SS families kept concentration camp prisoners as servants in their houses and gardens. So many people moved in, however, that the camp administration soon refused to assign any more living-space. In order to control this development, Höss decreed that special permission was required for any further visits.

Rudolf Höss lived with his wife Hedwig and, at first, four children (a fifth was born in 1943), only a hundred metres or so outside the camp grounds in a house that had belonged to the Polish administrator of the former military base. The 'first family' in the hierarchy of the SS settlement, the Höss family lived in thoroughly pleasant conditions. They were not affected by the economic misery of the region, because the commandant helped himself from the concentration camp stores – secretly and without paying.

In Auschwitz a wide variety of cultural events kept all the SS men in a good mood. Light entertainments, pleasant music and jolly gatherings provided distraction and amusement. Every two to three weeks events for the benefit of the troops took place in the old theatre building in the camp grounds. The camp administration set up its own concert wing, and theatre ensembles from Silesia and many of the towns in the Old Reich played for the SS. The entertainment offered extended from a theatrical genre called *Diebeskomödien* ('thief comedies') via cheerfully frivolous farces with titles like 'A Bride in Flight' and 'Disturbed Wedding Night', to 'Merry Variétés' and soirées under the motto 'Attack of the Comics'. And there was no shortage of classics in Auschwitz: in February 1943 the Dresden State Theatre presented a programme entitled 'Goethe Then and Now'.

The 'German House' on the Bahnhofsplatz was the local SS pub. Directly opposite the station, and reserved for Germans only, it served – from the beginning of 1941 it was known as the 'Waffen-SS House' (Waffen-SS: 'Armed SS') – both as a pub for the Lager-SS and as a hotel for high-ranking outside guests of the camp administration; female Jehovah's Witness prisoners were employed in the kitchen and as chambermaids. In the summer of 1943 preparations for a very special guest were made on the upper floor: Heinrich Himmler had his own apartment set up there, with a study, a bedroom and a bathroom. He never actually moved into this accommodation, but he clearly did intend to stay there for a lengthy period of time, because the plans for the apartment coincided with the time when Auschwitz was fast becoming the central showpiece of the 'Final Solution of the Jewish Question' within the state extermination programme – a development that the Reichsführer-SS clearly wanted to observe from close up.

Within the SS certain knowledge of the crimes in the camp was spreading. As the murder of the 'inferior peoples' ensured their own long-term future in the East, and the German claim to dominance provided ideological justification for such acts, the lives of the SS families and their conception of respectability and morality remained untouched by the murders. Domestic peace did not contradict the professional everyday life of the SS members. In fact the insistently nurtured family idyll may actually have encouraged the killing in the camp, because it gave the SS men the psychological stability they needed. We should not be surprised that SS men could be both mass murderers and loving fathers. The façade of family happiness revealed nothing whatsoever about the men's humanitarian convictions. Rather, the extermination of 'inferior' people was given moral legitimacy by the idea that it was securing the existence of the 'Aryan race', and against a background of a biological and genetic value system it was seen as entirely necessary. Mass murder and respectability were not opposites, but were closely interwoven. So to see mass crime as the result of pathological states of mind seems just as implausible as assuming that the perpetrators had fallen victim to a collective split personality. SS family life –

like mass extermination – served the construction of the 'racially pure' ethnic community. No one better summed up the National Socialist vision of ethics as an issue of racially ideological homogeneity than Heinrich Himmler, when at the beginning of October 1943, in the notorious speech to SS officers in Posnan, he declared that the SS had remained 'morally decent' in the mass murder of the European Jews. Himmler clad the unshakeable feeling of respectability in an unbearable dialectic which turned the murder of hundreds of thousands of people into the sentimental tragedy of the perpetrators.

3

Forced labour and extermination

IG Farben

In the spring of 1941 IG Farben (Interessen-Gemeinschaft Farbenindustrie AG) built a new factory in Auschwitz. The plant, called IG Auschwitz, was one of the biggest, most ambitious and, at a cost of about 600 million Reichsmarks, most expensive investment projects of the German Reich in the Second World War. IG Farben, founded in 1925 and with its headquarters in Frankfurt am Main, was, as a producer of synthetic substitute materials, important to the war effort, the most important private company in Nazi Germany and one of the biggest chemicals companies in Europe. The Auschwitz works, about 3 kilometres east of the Old Town, and about 7 kilometres away from the concentration camp, was to produce Buna, a kind of rubber synthetically manufactured from coal in support of the war effort.

IG Farben made Auschwitz the location of the new facility, its fourth site for Buna production after the works in Schkopau, Hüls and Ludwigshafen, at the end of lengthy discussions. It is not easy to say whether the determining factor was the concentration camp and the related possibility of cheap labour, or issues of geographical and economic location. There is much to suggest that the company management wanted to use the concentration camp as a source of labour, but that the existence of the camp was not the sole reason for the choice of location. The assured supply of raw materials and water, as well as helpful transport connections, also had a part to play.

Before the decision was made in Auschwitz's favour, other locations were discussed: in the autumn of 1939, after drawing up its four-year plan, the company had started building a Buna factory in Rattwitz near Breslau, and had already invested 4 million Reichsmarks in the project. But in the summer of 1940 building work was halted, because more attractive locations had been made available by the conquest of France. But after the failure of the air offensive against Britain, IG Farben revived the idea of building the Buna works in the conquered East. Though high investment costs were involved, the Reich Ministry of Economy forced through the plan and in return gave their agreement to the construction of another factory in Ludwigshafen. Lest it lost the monopoly on the manufacture of Buna, the company management agreed. So in the end the economic situation was less crucial than simple opportunism.

In early November 1940 it was quite clear that Silesia would be IG Farben's new production site. In the discussion of the future location the abandoned construction site at Rattwitz came under consideration, as well as three other sites in the Silesian Old Reich zone: Emilienhof near Gogolin, Groschowitz to the south of Oppeln, and Gross-Döbern to the north. During the initial phase of discussions, on the other hand, Auschwitz was not one of the potential locations. Otto Ambros, a member of the IG Farben board, did not suggest the town until the end of December 1940, on his return from a trip to Silesia. It is not clear how his attention was drawn to Auschwitz. He may have been trying to eliminate an important competitor, because the petroleum company Mineralölbau (Mineral Oil Construction) GmbH had developed plans to erect a hydration plant at the same time and was looking for a site near Auschwitz, the very plot of land in the administrative area of Dwory and Monowitz where the IG Farben factory would later be built. It is quite possible that Ambros beat the competing company to the factory location. The other sites, including Rattwitz, which had been preferred until that point, were no longer mentioned after the beginning of 1941. IG Farben favoured Auschwitz.

The terrain was sound, being level and flood-free. The necessary raw materials, coal, lime and water, were in abundant supply, the station was close at hand and supplies could be received. One other factor that may have been important to IG Farben was the financial support provided by the National Socialist state within the context of the Eastern Aid programme for the foundation of factories in the Eastern regions. This aspect of the settlement of the East, directly related to the assumption of territorial rights, was thus also crucial to the choice of location. The specific measures to encourage development immensely increased the attractiveness of the place. The Eastern Fiscal Assistance Law of December 1940 guaranteed IG Farben tax exemption on their investments. If the company directors had initially had concerns about the construction of a factory in the East on grounds of cost, the privileges they could expect from the Auschwitz site offered the prospect of soon recouping their outlay.

The company management contributed, to the cost of the indigenous population, to the safeguarding of economic and political domination in the occupied East. They came to Auschwitz with a spirit of racial superiority, and immediately began to reshape everything they found there. Helping the regime to fulfil its goals, but also acting to a remarkable degree on their own initiative, they accomplished not only the economic task entrusted to them, but beyond that also the 'racial' task of 'Germanizing' the East.

On 6 February 1941 Otto Ambros and IG Farben director Fritz ter Meer held a board meeting in Berlin with Carl Krauch, the plenipotentiary general for special questions of chemical production within the chemical industry, who was not only a member of the board of directors of IG Farben, but also a member of the circle of industrialists around the Reichsführer-SS, known as Himmler's 'Circle of Friends'. All three assumed that the work-force question could be solved by a 'large-scale settlement programme'. The link between industrialization and 'Germanization' was to a large extent institutionalized – which also meant moving out the indigenous Poles and Jews and bringing large numbers of Reich German workers to Auschwitz.

Krauch presented the plan to his close friend Hermann Göring, the head of the Four Year Plan authority. On

18 February 1941 Göring asked Himmler, in his role as Reich Commissar for the Strengthening of German Nationhood, to introduce pro-settlement measures as soon as possible, and to make concentration camp inmates available for the construction of the factory. On 26 February 1941 Himmler issued a ruling containing almost to the letter what the IG Farben company desired: he ordered the rapid expulsion of all Jews from the town of Auschwitz, decreed that all indigenous Poles who were capable of working should be left in the town and forced to work on the building of the IG Farben factory, and ordered that the greatest possible number of concentration camp prisoners be employed in the construction work.

Himmler's directive was the first special racial measure applied to Auschwitz because of the factory construction. The town was excluded from the region-specific settlement plans of East Upper Silesia, because IG Farben's building plan was such a significant project that new guidelines were passed for the redesign. Cooperation with the largest private company in the German Reich gave Himmler the unique chance to realize at last his desire to harness prisoner labour to economic ends, specifically in Upper Silesia, an area important for the munitions industry. Since the mid-thirties, the Reichsführer-SS had been trying to exploit the work-force of concentration camp inmates for munitions-related purposes in quarries, tile factories and gravel-pits, to ensure economic power for the SS, involve them in the production of munitions and build up their own armament production in the camps over the longer term. But these attempts were defeated by the lack of business experience among the SS and the low level of labour efficiency among the prisoners. Cooperation with IG Farben granted the opportunity to achieve those high goals.

On 1 March 1941, ten days after he had been informed of IG Farben's plans, Himmler travelled to Auschwitz for the first time. His interest is all the more striking in that he had barely shown the slightest interest in the concentration camp until that time, and had even called off a visit scheduled for October 1940. Himmler's visit led to crucial innovations: the camp administration assigned 10,000 prisoners to IG Farben, the first of whom were immediately put to work, and urgently applied for the distribution of material and the release of funds for the building of the factory. At the same time Commandant Höss intensified the annexation of the SS zone of interest. Expansion of the *Stammlager* ('parent camp') to a capacity of 30,000 prisoners pressed ahead. The construction of Birkenau camp, on the other hand, was not discussed. On his visit, Himmler merely issued orders concerning the settlement and agriculture projects, and planned future collaboration with IG Farben. The construction of Birkenau, which was to represent a further serious change in the functioning of the Auschwitz camp, and one that still could not be guessed at in the spring of 1941, was planned only a good six months later.

Intensive cooperation developed between IG Farben and the SS, and Otto Ambros immediately described it as a 'blessing'. The company contributed to the expansion of SS power, and the SS in turn emphatically supported the building of the factory. The company directors stressed the importance of speed. They planned a construction period of no more than three to four years, to be in production by mid-1943. The Reich Ministry of Economy assigned the project a building urgency level of zero, which was given only to projects important to the war effort. IG Farben immediately acquired the factory site in Dwory and Monowitz. Parts of the company grounds, which had belonged to Polish farmers and had been confiscated, were bought from state offices, and the rest was expropriated.

The founding meeting of IG Auschwitz was held on 7 April 1941. The invited guests, including senior SS representatives, listened to the address by Otto Ambros, who called the foundation of the factory a mission of settlement policy, and dramatically announced, given the great task facing them, that IG Farben would do anything in its power to advance the 'Germanization' of Auschwitz.

Monowitz and the sub-camps

IG Farben was the first private company to receive an army of prisoners as forced labourers. Their numbers rose from about 1,000 to twice that by the end of 1942. In 1943 there were 7,000 prisoners, and the peak of 11,000 was reached in 1944. Of about 35,000 working camp inmates more than 25,000 died as a result of their work for the chemicals giant.

Prisoners formed about a third of all workers in the

factory compound, along with thousands of forced *Fremd-arbeiter* ('foreign workers') from many European countries, which the company had acquired in cooperation with state authorities, among them Poles from East Upper Silesia and the General Government, as well as Dutchmen, Belgians, Yugoslavs, Russians, Frenchmen, Italians, Croats, Czechs, Greeks, Ukrainians, Britons and North Africans from Algeria and Morocco. The building site soon reached the size of an average-sized small town. The foreign workers were housed in barracks where, under close guard and divided by nationality, they were subjected to strict racial and hierarchical rules.

Difficulties involving the nature of the terrain, hold-ups in the deliveries of material and constant labour shortages slowed down the pace of building the new factory considerably. In the summer of 1942 the declared goal of starting production the following year was postponed to some remote date in the future. Against a background of underachievement by the prisoners that got worse and worse, the company management were spurred on by one particular project: 300 metres away from the building site, on the farmland belonging to the secluded village of Monowitz, a special concentration camp for the factory was to be built. At first the prisoners had been walking the 7 kilometres to the building site, which meant that their working day began at around three o'clock in the morning, and, once they had returned to the camp, ended much later than that of all the other inmates. As many of them arrived already exhausted at the building site in the morning, at the end of July IG Farben introduced a freight train for the prisoners between the parent camp and Dwory. When their work-levels still did not improve, the decision was made to build the Monowitz camp. IG Farben wanted to have at its disposal a source of cheap prisoners that it could use as it saw fit. A typhus epidemic slowed down the work, however, so that the first 2,000 prisoners were moved to the new camp, initially called 'Buna camp', only on 30 and 31 October 1942. It was the first concentration camp to be started and financed by a private company.

In Monowitz, food and so-called 'health care' were the responsibility of IG Farben. The camp was guarded by the SS, so that it resembled a state concentration camp even down to the smallest details. Watchtowers, a chicken-wire fence secured with barbed wire and an additional high-tension electric fence, illuminated at night, secured the camp. The site was larger than the parent camp's, but the barracks were smaller, more confined and just as overfilled. In mid-January 1943 the labour re-education camp in the parent camp was moved to Monowitz, the four barracks being separated by a fence; from that point onwards 're-education prisoners' were also sent to work on the factory building site.

From the point of view of company finance the prisoners' work unit was not profitable even once Monowitz had been built. Although the managers agreed with the SS that the average work capacity of a prisoner was 75 per cent that of a free German worker, this prognosis soon proved to be unrealistic. In fact the capacity of the prisoners clearly fell below 50 per cent of that of a German worker, and sometimes reached only 20 per

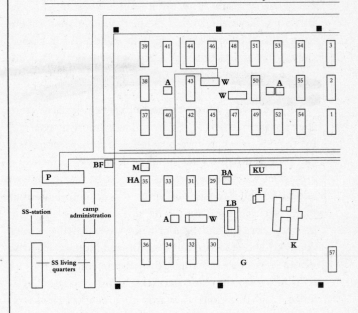

← to town of Auschwitz   *Grounds of IG Farben – Auschwitz*

| 39 | 41 | | 44 | 46 | 48 | 51 | 53 | 54 | | 3 |

| 38 | **A** | | 43 | | **W** | 50 | **A** | 55 | | 2 |
| | | | | **W** | | | | | |

| 37 | 40 | | 42 | 45 | 47 | 49 | 52 | 54 | | 1 |

BF

P

M
BA   **KU**
HA | 35 | 33 | 31 | 29 |

SS-station   **camp administration**

F

A   **W**   **LB**

SS living quarters

| 36 | 34 | 32 | 30 |

K

G   **57**

Monowitz (Buna) sub-camp

A   Latrine barracks
B   Bunkers and prison cells
BA Fire-fighting pool
BF Block leader's room
E   Electrical and mechanical workshop
G   Nursery
HA Prisoners' work unit
K   Prisoners' kitchen
KD Fumigation chamber
KO Central heating boiler
KU Smithy
LB Camp brothel

L   'Sauna' (bath) for patients from the prison infirmary and the mortuary
M   Barracks for the prisoners' orchestra
N   Tents where prisoners were housed when the barracks were over-full
P   SS staff estate
S   Stables
U   Temporary washing facility for prisoners housed in tents
W   Washrooms
■   Watchtower

MAP 4 *Monowitz (Buna) sub-camp – end 1944*

plant (Buna plant)   to Zator ⟶

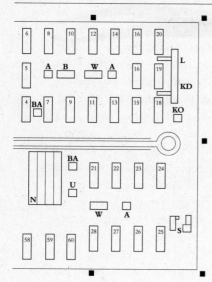

Building site for barracks for the new part of the camp

Prisoners' accommodation

  4   Prisoners' writing room, senior prisoners' dormitory and dormitory for the prisoners in the 'preferred' work unit

  1   Camp canteen and dormitory for the prisoners in the prisoners' orchestra

37–41   Section of the camp for re-education prisoners

 41   Outpatients' department and quarantine area for the re-education prisoners

 54   Clothes store

Prisoner's infirmary blocks

13   Block for convalescents (rest block)

14   Surgical department II

15   Internal medical department III and dental ward

16   Surgical department I

17   Internal medical department

18   Outpatient department and prisoners' infirmary office

19   Internal medical department I

20   Infectious diseases department

21   Block for convalescents (rest block)

cent. Despite the minimal labour costs, IG Farben made no profit out of the prisoners' units because productivity, given inadequate nutrition, harassment and punishments, and the physically draining and psychologically humiliating work, fell far short of expectations.

With the building of Monowitz camp IG Farben assumed an active role in the policy of the 'Final Solution'. Selections were made among the predominantly Jewish inmates – their proportion in the autumn of 1943 was between 60 and 75 per cent, and rose by early 1944 to about 90 per cent – as to those who were fit and unfit to work. The managers were convinced of the 'racial inferiority' of the prisoners. Being partly responsible for the escalation of the work unit policy, to a great extent – inasmuch as they perceived themselves as unimpeachable representatives of the German ruling class – they bore responsibility for the crimes. Their personal ambition to get the Buna works into operation despite a lack of time and a shortage of material forced them to be unscrupulous. The constant threat of transportation to Birkenau was a way of spurring on the prisoners to work. In pitiful living conditions and with minimal food, the life expectancy of the Monowitz inmates was on average about three months, and was often only a few weeks.

In exemplary fashion, IG Farben Auschwitz anticipated the links that were gradually forming between the SS and the munitions industry. The hiring out of prisoners to the company, begun in the spring of 1941, provided the model for systematically introducing forced labour in the war economy by the deployment of concentration camp inmates, and was organized by the newly founded central office for the efficient exploitation of the work-force represented by concentration camp prisoners, the SS Economic Administration Headquarters. Steelworks, companies in the chemicals and metals industries, as well as firms producing consumer goods settled near the Auschwitz camp from 1942, to follow the model of IG Farben in exploiting this cheap workforce. The SS charged 4 Reichsmarks for an unskilled labourer, 6 for a qualified worker; state industries were offered special deals, paying 4 Reichsmarks for qualified workers, and 3 Reichsmarks for unskilled labourers.

In August 1942 the Hermann Göring Works, one of the largest companies in the German Reich, settled in Auschwitz, followed in June 1943 by the Berg- und Hüttenwerkgesellschaft Teschen (Teschen Mining and Steelworks Company) and Energieversorgung Oberschlesien AG (Upper Silesian Energy Suppliers) and Friedrich Krupp AG. In October 1943 they were joined by the Weichsel Union Metallwerke (Vistula Union Metalworks), which took over the Krupp plant, and in December 1943 the Siemens–Schuckert factory moved in. The Reichsbahn ('Reich Railways') also employed camp inmates, as did various coalmines belonging to IG Farben, the Vereinigten Oberschlesischen Hüttenwerke (United Upper Silesian Steelworks), the Oberschlesischen Hydrierwerke (Upper Silesian Hydration Works), the Erdölraffinerie Trzebinia (Trzebinia Oil Refinery), the Vacuum Oil Company, the Deutschen Gasrußwerke, the Schlesischen Schuhwerke (Silesian Shoe Company) and the Schlesische Feinweberei (Silesian Textile Mill).

Barracks were built near or on the grounds of the private companies, so that – along with the camps of the SS-owned companies – a network of more than thirty sub-camps or camps external to the concentration camp came into being. Ten of them were built in the second half of 1944, and the last in December 1944, in Hubertushütte. The Auschwitz camp network included not just the wide area around the town of Auschwitz, but the whole of Upper Silesia, and also the Sudetenland (with one external camp) and the Reich Protectorate of Bohemia and Moravia (with two).

The number of Auschwitz prisoners in the German munitions industry was constantly on the rise; while there were around 6,000 in 1942, the number had trebled within a year. By the middle of 1944 there were, including the forced labourers brought in by IG Farben, around 42,000 prisoners. In their own companies in Auschwitz the SS employed about 8,500 prisoners. The most important and biggest of these was Deutsche Ausrüstungs-werke GmbH (German Equipment Company); the SS also ran the cement factory AG Golleschau, Deutsche Lebensmittel GmbH (German Food Company) and the Deutsche Erd- und Steinwerke GmbH (German Earth and Stoneworks). About half of the prisoners in SS companies, especially women, worked in the SS agricultural estate in the SS zone of interest, such as the Rajsko nursery, the Harmense fish and poultry breeding plant and in Babitz, Budy, Birkenau and Plawy, where sub-camps were also built; in addition, women worked in the demolition of buildings, building roads and digging ditches in the zone of interest.

Living and working conditions in the sub-camps were no better than they were in the other parts of the camp. Hunger, hard work and ruthless exploitation were a fact of everyday life. The inmates often worked for fifteen hours and more. Some sub-camps, including Blechhammer, Trzebinia, Lagischa and Jawischowitz, as well as the coalmines, were considered murderous for unskilled workers. Only qualified workers were slightly better off, since they were hard to replace and thus escaped being assigned from the outset to lethal work duties.

Until the administrative restructuring of the camp complex all the sub-camps, including Monowitz, were under the leadership of the administration of the parent camp. On 22 November 1943 the replacement of Commandant Rudolf Höss, the reasons for which are not precisely known, led to a change in the organization of the camp; Höss was succeeded by SS-Obersturmbannführer Arthur Liebehenschel. Höss took over his job as director of the headquarters of the SS Economic Administration Central Office in Berlin–Oranienburg, and he was thus promoted to the post of deputy to the inspector of concentration camps. With the change at the top of the administration, the camp area was divided into three administratively separate and autonomous complexes: Auschwitz I, the parent camp; Auschwitz II, i.e. Birkenau camp, which encompassed the SS's own agricultural sub-camp, and was so vast that SS 'protective custody camp leaders' were employed for the individual camp sections; and Auschwitz III, the sub-camp conglomerate, the largest individual camp of which was Monowitz.

Each of the three camps had its own SS administrative authority with a commandant at its head: Liebehenschel was commandant of the parent camp, and after his transfer to the same position at the Majdanek camp near Lublin he was succeeded in May 1944 by SS-Sturmbannführer Richard Baer. The commandant of Auschwitz–Birkenau was SS-Obersturmbannführer Friedrich Hartjenstein, and from May 1944 SS-Hauptsturmführer Josef Kramer. A further organizational turning point, in November 1944, saw the transformation of Monowitz into an autonomous concentration camp, from then on the administrative centre of all the sub-camps. The commandant of Auschwitz III, and later also of Monowitz as well as the sub-camps, was SS-Hauptsturmführer Heinrich Schwarz.

The principle of 'selection'

The regular removal of prisoners according to criteria of economic usefulness, which had at first been sporadically employed in the spring of 1942, became the rule from 4 July 1942. On that day the first selection of a whole transport began among Slovakian Jews. This date marks the beginning of systematic extermination. From now on the selection, made by SS doctors and other functionaries, determined whether prisoners lived or died. The victims included all those prisoners who were excluded from labour deployment because of their physical constitution: children, pregnant women, old people, sick people and the handicapped.

Those selected for work – in Auschwitz on average

about 20 per cent of a prisoner transport – were exposed to the harshest conditions. In the arsenal of methods of killing, forced labour was only one means among others, labour deployment was only a synonym for a slower death. After an average of three to four months most of the prisoners forced to work were dead, having succumbed to beatings and hunger, weakness and inhuman living conditions.

'Extermination through work' – the phrase appears in a letter from Reich Justice Minister Otto Georg Thierack to Himmler written on 18 September 1942 – was not a concept programmatically developed and systematically put into action, but a stage in the murder programme: temporarily excused extermination were those who could work to make up for the labour shortage of the German Reich, which had become very striking since the German army's crisis on the edge of Moscow. At the same time, high death-rates did not damage economic interests, because further supplies of employable workers were always guaranteed by the steady flow of prisoner transports to Auschwitz.

None the less, labour deployment was just as much aimed at realizing the racial dogma of physical extermination as were mass shootings and murder in the gas chambers – but in a form that was profitable to the economy of the German Reich. The labour deployment of prisoners was the result of racist policy, not contrary to it; not the antithesis of extermination but a bridge to mass murder.

4

Auschwitz the 'model town'

The bulwark of the German presence in the East

If, belonging as it did to the 'Eastern strip', which was inferior from the point of view of territorial rights, Auschwitz had originally played a marginal part in the Nazi 'Germanization policy', its significance was fundamentally transformed in the spring of 1941 with the construction of the IG Farben plant. The town now enjoyed a peculiarly special status within the settlement of East Upper Silesia: Auschwitz was the 'model of Eastern settlement'. The town became the ideal of economic annexation and racial selection, the future model of German rule in the conquered country, in short, a 'bulwark of the German presence in the East'. The policy of linking industrialization, urban improvement and population restructuring was brutally driven forward. Not only in the spring of 1942, as was projected for the 'Eastern strip', but as early as April 1941 Jews were deported from the town of Auschwitz, the former Jewish collection point, and indigenous Poles were forced into their districts, with their poor infrastructural connections.

To encourage an entrepreneurial spirit and attract

capital, as well as to tempt independent craftsmen, farmers and freelances to the East, the National Socialist state offered generous enticements in terms of finance and living conditions. There was the prospect of income tax relief, citizens' tax was lower than it was in the Old Reich, and because of the 'Eastern exemption' there was hardly any property tax. There were also special terms for credit, as well as child benefit and marriage loans.

On 3 April 1941, the beginning of the week of Pesach, the mass deportation of the Jewish inhabitants of the town began – and continued for a whole week. Over the course of those days a ghostly procession was set in motion, from the Old Town towards the station. Five Reichsbahn trains were required to transport the Jews away; the old and the sick travelled on horse-drawn carts. The Jews were brought to large-scale collection points about 30 kilometres away; more than 3,000 went to Sosnowitz, and about 2,000 to Bendzin (Bendsburg). Those among them who were capable of work were handed over to the office responsible for Jewish forced-labour deployment in East Upper Silesia under SS-Brigadeführer Albrecht Schmelt.

The few Jews who lived in 'mixed marriages' with Catholics were at first allowed to remain in the town, as were the members of the Jewish Council, some fifty people in all, who had to clear the Jewish apartments on behalf of the town's German administration. Once they had finished doing that, however, they too were trans-ported to the collection points. The cleared apartments were left locked and bolted for their future German inhabitants. The synagogue had already been destroyed by the Gestapo in November 1939, small Jewish prayer-houses in Auschwitz were now turned into storehouses, the hospital and other welfare institutions were closed. Within a short time the Jewish community had ceased to exist. The force of the intervention changed the town completely. The building of the IG Farben plant brought the tradition of the former 'Oświęcim Jerusalem', more than 700 years old, to an abrupt end. The plant managers were not to be cheated of the opportunity to witness the revolution that they had unleashed. Many of them lined the streets during the deportations, and it was certainly no coincidence that the founding session of the factory took place two days before they ended. Immediately after the transport of the Jews the town of Auschwitz broke away from the 'Eastern strip', inferior both racially and in terms of territorial rights, and the police border drawn within the town at the beginning of the war disappeared. Auschwitz received the same status as towns in the western, 'racially valuable' part of the Reich district of Kattowitz.

Nothing more is known about the fate of the Jews of Auschwitz. It is unclear how they lived in the collection centres of Sosnowitz and Bendzin, which were soon closed off into ghettos, and neither is it clear how many were later murdered in the camp at the gates of their own town. Finally, we do not know whether or to what extent the deportations were accompanied by a spirit of anti-Semitism. We have no information about the reactions of the town's Polish inhabitants. Presumably they responded to the deportations with indifference. Apart from the social privileges enjoyed by IG Farben,

Poles were also threatened with deportation as soon as they had finished serving as workers in the building of the factory. Since March 1941 they had also been vulnerable to the rigid legal and social system of the German *Volksliste* ('ethnic list'), which reduced the social and political status of many of them after racial and ethnic investigation. The social status of the Poles depended on the degree of their individual capacity to 'become German' or 'revert to being German'; Jews were excluded from this pattern from the outset. The *Volksliste* procedure, introduced by Himmler in the annexed Eastern regions, brought together nationality, the principle of descent and racial criteria. The purpose of the selection was to comb the Polish population for 'people of German blood', to preserve a 'racially valuable' asset for the German nation. The procedure distinguished between four 'ethnic groups' and 'national' political achievements, and on that basis four classes of nationality with different rights. This classification not only decided a person's status, but also determined property rights, economic security and social position. Most of the Polish inhabitants of Auschwitz did not enjoy the social and legal superiority of the three *Volksliste*-classified groups, but were seen as so-called *Schutzangehörige* ('protected dependants'), an inferior class separate from the Germans and without rights of any kind.

As a consequence of the deportations, by the spring of 1941 the town was half depopulated. Of the 7,600 inhabitants about 90 per cent were Poles, and the rest were German or of German descent. The governing class was formed of exactly 600 Reich Germans and ethnic Germans; they quickly established themselves as the beneficiaries of the revolution.

National Socialist plans for the future

At breakneck speed an industry-led urbanization policy began. Its goal was to modernize housing conditions in Auschwitz, in order to entice a qualified German work-force and its families out of the Old Reich. IG Farben saw the building of new houses and improved transport connections as the most important conditions for the fulfilment of their racial task.

The factory management's interest was concentrated on comfortable accommodation and quality of life, and nothing repelled them as much as the state of the streets and houses. The staff arriving in the supposedly cul-turally backward town were to find well-equipped and child-friendly apartments as well as all kinds of sport and leisure institutions. The plan to conjure up a modern town with public buildings, extensive transport connec-tions and many green spaces was based on the arbitrary exercise of power and delusions of grandeur. None the less many plans were worked out to the smallest detail, and some of them were actually realized. A number of different agencies were authorized to contribute to the Reich housing policy, and many of these sent representa-tives to Auschwitz, where they spent days and weeks discussing designs, visiting locations and rebuilding the town. The concentration camp, later an extermination camp, clearly disturbed no one, either aesthetically or politically. The close connection between the town and the IG Farben factory was characteristic of the re-design of Auschwitz. The town became dependent on IG Farben, relying on it for the supply of electricity and heating, and even the water came from the factory well.

As the major financier of the town's modernization, IG Farben bore the costs not only of the factory's own 'staff estate', but also for the urbanization of 'Auschwitz the residential town'. The Reich authorities supported the plan with generous loans. The company put in its own capital and had considerable influence on the new building plans. Its own company, Gewoge, responsible for building the housing of the factory employees, shared the organization and financing of the projects with Neue Heimat ('New Homeland'), which had a branch in Kattowitz and was responsible, on behalf of the German Labour Front, for building housing in the town. The plans reflected a high level of technology and 'modern-ity': 1,600 'people's dwellings', as they were called, were planned at first, each between 60 and 90 square metres in area, and also single-family houses and maisonettes with vegetable gardens and garages. Central heating and a hot-water supply were just as natural a part of domestic comfort as heating and gas technology, and each house had a laundry. The plans were constantly extended, projects tirelessly expanded, and several hundred apart-ments in the 'IG staff estate' were actually built; now they are part of the 'chemists' estate' of Oświęcim.

The Reich ministries, including the Reich Ministry of Labour and the Reich Ministry of Economy, placed large

amounts of money at the disposal of the 'model settlement town' of Auschwitz. Almost every single applica-
tion for state subsidy was accepted, and almost all the
'Old Town renovation measures' were put through –
and this in the middle of the war and despite all state
economy drives. Like the IG Farben plant, all the
town-building measures were given the highest level of
urgency in the grant hierarchy of the general plenipotentiary for house-building. Construction was never
halted in Auschwitz, and the flow of money was never
interrupted.

The chief figure in the modernization of the town was
Hans Stosberg, a qualified architect and business director
of an architectural office in Breslau. At the end of
December 1940 he had been given the job, by the district
planning department of Upper Silesia, of drawing up
plans for the reorganization and development of Auschwitz. As head architect of the 'model settlement town',
Stosberg was given extensive powers: he negotiated on
behalf of the municipality with IG Farben, as well as the
regional and super-regional authorities. Stosberg, who
designed countless plans and maquettes for Auschwitz,
devoted himself to the new building project and realized
his vision of modern town planning. With a grand sense
of historical purpose, and inspired by the racial task
before him, he was no more repelled than anyone else
by the concentration and extermination camp. For New
Year 1942 he sent greetings cards with the proud statement: 'Birth of the new German town of Auschwitz'.

Stosberg's plans represented the powerful self-image
of the Nazi regime. Following the principle of the 'urban

landscape', which was for Himmler the 'leading formal and aesthetic idea of the time', Auschwitz was to become the model of the National Socialist 'ethnic community' in terms of town planning as well. Stosberg planned for the town to be divided into cell-shaped districts with monumental community buildings, parade grounds, showpiece buildings and Party assembly rooms, with homes for the Hitler Youth, leisure amenities and local Party meeting rooms. He planned an imposing avenue with wide rows of houses branching off it. Monstrous ideas were set out on the drawing board. Whole satellite towns and new districts were planned. A straight road from the station through the middle of the Old Town to the IG Farben factory would require the removal of the sixteenth-century Catholic church of the Assumption. The lack of proportion evident in these projects (which were only partially realized) is apparent in the plans for the public institutions: Stosberg planned twelve schools, six kindergartens, twenty playing-fields and several additional stadiums with swimming-pools and playing-fields. The centre of the town was Alt-Auschwitz ('Old Auschwitz'), with government offices, banks, shops and the market square. With Neustadt-Ost and Neustadt-West ('New Town East/West'), autonomous town centres would arise, with Party buildings, wide roads, the SS estate and a housing estate for employees of the Reichsbahn. And if the town could not accommodate the building projects, there were two 'reserve zones' available in the neighbouring parishes of State-Stawy and Zaborze.

The Jewish quarter of the town of Auschwitz had

ceased to exist in the plans. The Jewish cemetery, which had been abandoned since the deportation of the Jews, was to make way for a Party building with a hotel, a cinema and a restaurant. The gravestones had already been used for road-building at the beginning of the redevelopment. In his maquette the chief architect grouped around the nucleus of the Old Town, according to Stosberg the 'symbol of the medieval German settler spirit', the Piast castle, the market square and the town hall. In his drawings, the town centre was adorned with leafy Silesian lanes, and there were even a fountain in the marketplace and lime trees, and a little tower on top of the town hall.

The management of IG Farben at first assumed a work-force of 3,000 Reich Germans, then 5,500, but this figure soon rose to about 15,000. As plans progressed, the figures mounted. In June 1941 Stosberg had anticipated a total work-force of 30,000, but this soon rose, first to 40,000, then to 60,000 and finally, in the 'ideal plan' of January 1943, to between 70,000 and 80,000 people.

The plans were pursued even when Stosberg, after two and a half years of work on the project, was called up to the Wehrmacht in September 1943; a district building officer now took over his tasks.

During the development of the town, Party and civilian authorities never came into conflict with the SS over the crimes in the camp. Instead, arguments tended to break out over the political competition for land and areas of influence, because the vast town development plans came into conflict with the concentration camp's extension projects, which the Lager-SS were designing at the same time. They argued over the issue of whether the left or the right bank of the Soła marked the border between the town and the camp, and whether the SS would build a sewage treatment plant where the Soła branched off from the Vistula, or the civilian authorities would set up a central water supply complex on the same site. The question of the extent to which the SS zone of interest would penetrate the land belonging to the town, and whether Oppeln would be drawn into the station extension by the directors of the Reichsbahn, was an additional source of conflict. In order to clear up the issue of the regional boundary, late in September 1942, in the Waffen-SS building, Himmler called a meeting between representatives of the SS Economic Administration Central Office, Lager-SS, IG Farben and the provincial and urban administration, at which he was represented by Oswald Pohl, the head of the SS Economic Administration Office. The debate reached a grotesque climax at a meeting in Berlin in January 1943, when representatives of the civilian authorities demanded the transfer of the SS zone of interest for reasons of landscape design. The concentration camp, they suggested, should be rebuilt somewhere else, where it would fit less 'inorganically' into its surroundings.

When the boundary was definitively fixed in June 1943, this established the administrative autonomy of the SS zone of interest. Himmler thus achieved his goal of withdrawing the camp compound from the formal administrative control of the civilian administration, and making it the sole responsibility of the SS. With the agreement of the civilian authorities the SS zone of interest now became an official district in its own right. The commandant of the parents camp – and this was unique among the commandants of the concentration camps throughout the Reich – received the rank of *Amtskommissar* ('Official Commissar'), comparable to the office of mayor, and was thus awarded certain powers in the civilian administration. Both Höss, who had already been a member of the Labour Chamber in the *Gau* of Upper Silesia since 1941, and his successors Liebehenschel and Baer acted as *Amtskomissare*, and the guard unit of the Waffen-SS acted as a police force in the SS zone of interest.

The town of Auschwitz drew certain advantages from its connection with the SS, because the fixing of the boundary delivered the privilege it had long desired of a German *Gemeindeordnung* ('community law'). The bestowal of this privilege demonstrated that the process of 'Germanization' was almost concluded, as did the new town coat of arms: an eagle with a large 'A' on its chest, standing proudly on the medieval Piast castle: the innocent symbol of the town of mass extermination.

Mass crimes and the civilian population

By October 1943 more than 6,000 Reich Germans had moved to Auschwitz. The first to settle there were mostly officials working in the newly created town offices, the Schutzpolizei ('Security Police') were reinforced, and in January 1943 the new Gestapo office moved into the former vicarage of the church of the

Assumption. Craftsmen and businessmen were also among the new arrivals, but most came to Auschwitz as workers and employees of the IG Farben works. The bulk of the new inhabitants moved from towns where the company had its main factories: Ludwigshafen, Hüls, Leuna and Frankfurt am Main. Both men and women were drawn to Auschwitz, and there was a high proportion of young people, clearly carrying out part of their training in the new factory. Generally, at first, existing employees of IG Farben came, and their families followed in the course of time. It is not clear what criteria were employed in choosing the workers for the Auschwitz plant; political reliability as well as specialist qualifications might have played an important role, and, in the service of securing the ethnic German future, age must have played a part as well.

Despite the future development programme for the town, living conditions remained difficult, and un-attractive to the German inhabitants.

Neither the water supply nor sewage disposal were properly sorted out. Because of insanitary conditions, spotted fever, dysentery and typhus flourished. From the start of 1942 the camp administration forbade SS men and their families to enter the town, lest they bring disease back into the camp. And accommodation was uncertain as well, because housing in the IG staff estate was still being built and factory workers often had to move into houses and apartments a long way away.

But the Reich Germans were not deterred, and their numbers actually rose when the air raids over the Old Reich became more severe in the second half of 1943.

Auschwitz, in the Reich's Silesian 'air raid shelter', was for a long time spared attacks from the air. But in July and August 1943 the town residents' report office recorded 2,400 moves to Dwory and a further 650 to the villages around Auschwitz. By now German settlers were no longer coming only from towns where IG Farben had bases, but from all part of the Old Reich, from Hamburg, Essen, Cologne, Münster, Magdeburg and Munich, and even from Vienna.

Nowhere in the twenty-four towns in the district of Bielitz was the number of new Reich German citizens higher than it was in Auschwitz. The settlers were distinguished by a pioneering spirit, a belief in the future, their efforts to bring 'German culture' to the East, as well as a high level of business efficiency. Concentrating on their livelihoods, they were indifferent to the camp; but they did notice its existence when, for example, the Lager-SS, on Wehrmacht Day at the end of March 1943, invited them to a 'communual feast followed by entertainments in the afternoon'.

The fact that the private lives of the Reich Germans in Auschwitz remained untouched by mass murder is also demonstrated by the noisy New Year festival in 1943, which German residents celebrated in the Ratshof pub in the market square, the first building in the square. The landlord and hotelier, who had moved to the town from Wuppertal, wrote to a friend in the Old Reich to tell him about the preparations: tickets were as much in demand as for 'the press ball in Berlin'. In the middle of the war – and in full view of the camp – 200 Reich German guests supped heartily on goose liver and oxtail soup, blue carp in aspic, roast hare and biscuit roulade, Sekt and pancakes, and in the early hours of the morning there was herring salad and coffee. The festivities were cordial, there was dancing, a master of ceremonies from Vienna guided everyone through the evening, a dance-band played, and a comedian entertained the room.

Unaffected by events in the camp, garden designers, landscape architects and botanists turned Auschwitz into an experimental research zone. As a fanatical nature-worshipper, Himmler wanted to see procedures for recycling refuse and sewage, for biological waste processing, the growth of plant cultures and technical innovations in the use of slurry and composting. In the shadow of the gas chambers these projects became reality. Among the visitors who came several times to Auschwitz was Heinrich Wiepking-Jürgensmann, professor of landscape and garden design at the agricultural college in Berlin, and also special representative for landscape design and landscape care in the staff headquarters of the Reich Commission for the Strengthening of German Nationhood. Employed in an advisory capacity in the development of landscape design in the annexed Eastern regions, he was deeply involved with projects in Auschwitz; one of his students wrote a dissertation on the redesign of the town.

The people who were aware of the details of mass extermination, apart from the SS leadership, were above all the employees of the Reichsbahn who directed the freight trains carrying Jews from the whole of Europe to Birkenau. In the timetables of the Reichsbahn the transports were listed as special passenger trains, but were *de facto* sent out as goods trains. The client was the Reichssicherheitshauptamt, or RSHA (sometimes represented by regional Gestapo offices), but the process was overseen by the Reich Transport Ministry. The Reichsbahn had the journey paid for as traditional freight transport. The money came from the victims themselves, who had to buy a third-class ticket for their journey to the death camp: 4 pfennigs per person for every kilometre of track; for children under the age of ten, 2 pfennigs. The Reichsbahn granted the SS a group rebate – half-price for transports of 1,000 people or more – and the empty train journeys on the way back were free, surely one of the most breathtaking details of the organization of mass murder.

There was a great deal of effort involved, because when a train arrived at Auschwitz station it had first to be shunted into a siding. The locomotives were swapped over, and the railway staff took over the carriages. A team of three, sometimes four, officials accompanied the transports to the camp. The railwaymen were present when the SS drove the inmates out of the carriages. They saw the selection process, watched the prisoner units unloading the luggage and the columns going to the crematoria. They brought the empty carriages back to the station, where the duty foreman of the goods dispatch office was already waiting for them.

Attacks on trains and railway lines on the stretch to Auschwitz increased after 1943, presumably deliberate acts by Polish resistance fighters, trying to stop or at least to hinder the prisoner transports. Tracks were loosened and freight trains derailed, locomotives and carriages blown off the line by explosive devices. The attacks reached such a pitch that Germans no longer felt safe in the area around Auschwitz – and began to apply for gun licences.

When corpses were found along the tracks, the authorities assumed that they were Jews. The gendarmerie made no further inquiries, and the Lager-SS had the bodies removed. The finding of corpses provoked horror among the general public, but less and less the more frequently such findings occurred. The fact that passengers rose from their seats and crossed to the windows when Birkenau camp could be seen in the distance suggests that it gave them a certain thrill.

Partial information, rumours and suppositions circulated among the civilian population of Auschwitz. People suspected the worst when they noticed the sweetish smell of burning flesh, too pungent to be ignored – though anyone who wanted to could find reassuring explanations for it; for example, there was quite naturally a high mortality rate in the camp, and the corpses had to be incinerated. Certainly, there was a latent anxiety which meant that no one asked any questions. The grimmest suspicions were forced to the back of people's minds by everyday concerns and private matters. Indifference was everywhere apparent; how far people agreed with what was happening is unclear. But any protests were muted; quiescence was far more typical.

After the end of the war railway employees said they knew nothing of the mass extermination until 1943. But no one had asked to be moved to another location because, they said, they did not have the enthusiasm to do so, and they thought they were doing a valuable job. Their indifference meant the railwaymen could go about their murderous business as if it were quite routine. Out of a sense of obedience, and also stamped by the pedantic precision of their profession, they showed no misgivings about their own actions. That the burden of knowing about the systematic killing that was happening had no consequences for them shows how people were able to come to terms with mass murder.

5

The 'Final Solution of the Jewish Question'

Extermination policy

What Himmler, Reich Commissar for the Strengthening of German Nationhood, proudly called a 'modern mass migration', and began to put into effect without any restraint; what, in the language of the German occupying forces, with utter contempt for humanity, was known as 'the removal of human ballast' and 'racial cleansing'; and what, in the official reports from the offices of the Reich Commissar, was listed under 'significant population-related structural cleansing' was the brutal uprooting and violent expulsion of hundreds of thousands of people. The deportation programme was not a military experiment undertaken by irrational fantasists. Rather, based on sound power-political interests, it formed the defining political and ideological leitmotif of German policy in conquered Poland. The 'new racial order' was aimed at moving masses of 'alien' and 'racially good' human beings back and forth, regrouping them, resettling, settling and repatriating them, in order, in the name of 'bringing in valuable German blood', to usher in the victory of the 'Aryan' race over Jews and Slavs.

The planners in the RSHA did not react to drawbacks

in the settlement programme by reducing 'evacuation quotas', or by extending the planning period, but rather by insistently pushing ahead with their campaign. Obstacles were overcome 'maximally', which is to say in the most radical way imaginable. Inherent necessities were created that made it possible to continue the deportation programme as before, despite growing difficulties. A process of continuous radicalization came into operation, given concrete form in strategic plans of increasingly immoderate scope.

The 'Final Solution of the Jewish Question' cannot be separated from the context of the racist Eastern policy any more than it can be from the resettlement programme of the 'ethnic Germans' from eastern and southern Europe. Radicalized to an extreme degree, the dynamic of resettlement and settlement in the service of racial restructuring led to the systematic mass murder of the Jews, even if that had not been the goal of the plans from the outset. 'Resettlement', 'clearance' and 'evacuation' were, between 1939 and 1941, still meant literally, and only gradually became synonyms for mass murder.

After earlier economic and logistical delays, military priorities put a definitive end to systematic population restructuring on 15 March 1941, when the Russian campaign which would tie up all resources ceased to be compatible with ethnic-policy operations. Until that point ethnic-policy measures in conquered Poland had been directed against both Jews and Poles. Their goal was to clear the territories that were to be settled by Germans of 'alien ethnicities', to make room for ethnic

Germans and Reich Germans. Earlier instances of expropriation and disenfranchisement had involved expulsion and deportation, but not killing.

For the removal of the Jews to ghettos and extermination camps the procedures carried out during the settlement operations were of crucial importance, because the development of the human transports as an administrative act – with precise timetables, cost calculations and contingency plans – was already routine long before the systematic murder of the Jews began. The division of labour, demarcation of duties and the fragmentation of responsibility were established as basic structural principles in the policy of extermination.

On 22 June 1941, when Hitler attacked the Soviet Union, his goal was to defeat his enemy in a *Blitzkrieg* ('lightning war'), to secure Germany's lasting hegemony in Europe and finally to realize the national utopia of '*Lebensraum* in the East'. In the climate of victory euphoria and political megalomania, the regime set its course against ideological enemy number one: the Jews. If the strategists of the previous resettlement policy had had to accept that their plans would face stagnation, checks and dead-ends, the vision of the conquest of the Soviet Union opened up a new dimension to the racial New Order of Europe. The radicalization of anti-Jewish policies took its course with unheard-of brutality.

The goal of the 'liberation of *Lebensraum* in the East', the strategic guiding principle that the head of the RSHA, Reinhard Heydrich, had worked out at the end of March 1941 on Hitler's behalf, was the transfer of the Jews from the German sphere of power into the conceptually and geographically nebulous East. The principle of forced deportation still prevailed in the sense of the 'territorial final solution', but the death of the victims, in contrast to earlier clearance projects, was factored in as a fixed planning dimension. The Jews were to be driven to Siberia or towards the Arctic Ocean, where they would die of supposedly natural causes: they would starve or freeze or fall victim to the murderous policy of forced labour.

Exile and extermination were interlinked, and became the means sanctioned by Nazi racial policy to 'make room for German people' in the conquered area. In connection with the radicalized programme of 'Germanization' of the East, anti-Jewish policy acquired its true impetus.

The plan for the systematic murder of the European Jews was, to all appearances, not the result of a single 'order', but the product of a lengthy decision-making process, which found concrete form in autumn 1941, and was then put in motion step by step, before being systematically completed in the early summer of 1942. Not so much directed from above as the result of a gradually radicalized policy, intensified to an extreme, that probably came into being spasmodically, in a process of 'cumulative radicalization' (Hans Mommsen), mass murder was equally influenced by complex plans and actions that had already been carried out. Hitler, although his role in this cannot be clearly and individually explained in detail, acted as the most senior moral and political legitimizing authority for it. The *Führer* granted his inferiors, in the polycratic system of government of the Nazi state, room for manoeuvre, to develop and realize their own plans autonomously, so that the decisive impetus in the implementation of the Final Solution came from regional initiatives. These initiatives on the part of lower-ranking bodies, and the administrative perfectionism of the Berlin headquarters, merged in the end into a criminal extermination programme.

The course was set towards genocide in the summer of 1941. The ideological equation of Bolshevism and Jewry both gave the impetus to and legitimized anti-Jewish policy. The SS and the police were given instructions to shoot Russian Jews 'in Party and state positions', and to encourage pogroms. The 'solution of the Jewish question' was to some extent improvised: in Lithuania, from July 1941 onwards, the units under the higher orders of Himmler and Heydrich shot Jewish men, women and children without distinction. Mass liquidations also occurred in Belorussia, in the western Ukraine, in Serbia and in the district of Galicia in the General Government. In the Warthegau functionaries within the civilian apparatus of occupation expressly factored in murder as part of their 'policy towards the Jews'. Large sections of the Wehrmacht implemented and supported the policy of murder.

In the Old Reich the deportation of the Jews began in the autumn of 1941, particularly from the large cities, but also from the Ostmark (annexed Austria) and the protectorate of Bohemia and Moravia. The Jews were to disappear on Hitler's wishes, and the Old Reich was to be *judenfrei* ('Jew-free') by the end of 1941. The obligatory wearing of the Star of David (the *Judenstern*), the prohibition on emigration and the removal of German nationality became part of the administrative preparations for deportation in autumn 1941. Trains holding some 20,000 Jews rolled into the already overcrowded ghetto of Łódź from mid-October 1941. In Minsk, Kaunas and Riga Jews were shot immediately upon arrival.

But the mass executions proved to be impracticable, since in view of the great numbers of victims it was hardly possible to organize them, let alone keep them secret; the men in the execution squads also complained of 'mental and nervous strain'. In mid-August 1941, on a visit to Minsk, Himmler ordered that alternative methods of killing be tried out. Experiments at killing the mentally handicapped were undertaken using explosives and poison gas. This all clearly demonstrates one thing: the regime was busy trying to find a means of murder that was as efficient as it was discreet and anonymous – and which minimized the psychological burden on those carrying out the executions.

It is difficult to place the Wannsee Conference (first planned for 9 December 1941, but deferred to 20 January 1942 after the USA entered the war) in the decision-making process concerning the 'Final Solution of the Jewish Question'. This meeting of the representatives of the ministerial authorities, the National Socialist Party and the SS apparatus, organized by Heydrich, served the cause of the administrative coordination of mass murder. Its purpose was to organize the division of labour, to integrate and assign roles to the various offices that would implement the programme of murder. That 'Lebensraum in the East is the solution' was set down as the guiding principle for future plans, and the policy of selection into those who were and those who were not able to work was established. Heydrich managed to demonstrate his competence as a coordinator of the 'Final Solution', and to confirm the practice of murder at a bureaucratic level. But the systematic murder of the Jews was not decided at Wannsee, because at the time of the conference the shootings in the Soviet Union were already under way, and other methods of killing had been under discussion for a long time.

In autumn 1941 – presumably because the war was not going as planned, because a speedy victory had failed to materialize, because rapid deportations were not possible and the German army was suffering setbacks – the occupied Soviet Union fell out of consideration as a prime site for murder within the context of the plans for a 'New Order' under Germany's Jewish policy, although mass shootings continued to take place, and plans for the construction of an extermination camp in the Belorussian town of Mogilev existed, which we must suppose were not put into effect because of the war situation. The geographical focus of the extermination of the Jews was transferred to the west, to the politically and militarily secured former Poland, where between late autumn 1941 and spring 1942 all mass extermination camps were set up: Chelmno, Bełżec, Sobibór, Treblinka, Majdanek and Auschwitz–Birkenau.

The extermination camps differed fundamentally from the concentration camps in both administrative and functional terms. While concentration camps served as places of imprisonment, and of re-education through terror, punishment and economic exploitation, as well as being training-grounds for the SS, the extermination camps had only a single purpose: the swift murder of the prisoners who arrived there. Auschwitz–Birkenau and Majdanek, which were both concentration camps and extermination camps, were special forms of these.

Chelmno in the Warthegau, which, like Auschwitz, belonged to the German Reich, was the first extermination camp. From 7 December 1941 Jews from the Łódź ghetto were murdered there, and later also Roma from the Burgenland and other non-Jews, 152,000 people in all. In March 1943 Chelmno was temporarily closed, but the following year, when the Łódź ghetto was destroyed, the mass murder there began all over again.

In Bełżec, Sobibór and Treblinka, the Operation Reinhard camps under the supervision of SS and police chief Odilo Globocnik, some 1.75 million Jews were murdered between the spring of 1942 and autumn 1943. Bełżec, in the district of eastern Galicia on the border of the district of Lublin, was ready for operation after a five-month building period in March 1943, and Sobibór in May 1942 and Treblinka in July 1942, both after about eight weeks of construction. In Bełżec, by the time of its closure in December 1942, around 600,000 Jews from the south-east Polish districts of the General Government had died. In Sobibór, on the eastern border of the district of Lublin, by August 1943 between 200,000 and 250,000 Jews from the district of Lublin, the Old Reich and various European countries had been killed. In Treblinka, east of Warsaw, between 750,000 and 900,000 Jews from the Warsaw district died, most of them from the ghetto, and also Jews from Białystok, Lublin, Radom, Bulgaria and Greece. Hardly anyone survived the Operation Reinhard camps: no more than fifty-four prisoners survived Treblinka, and only three Jews are believed to have managed to escape Bełżec.

In Majdanek mass murder began in August 1942. Of a total of some 180,000 victims between 50,000 and 120,000 were Jews, most of them from the district of Lublin, but many from Slovakia, Bohemia and Moravia, the Old Reich, Hungary, France, Belgium, the Netherlands and Greece, and also from Warsaw and Białystok. Except in Auschwitz, they were murdered with carbon monoxide.

Experiments in killing

The first mass killings in Auschwitz were not yet a part of the systematic policy to murder the European Jews. Rather they took place in the context of the experiments of the SS, the so-called 'euthanasia programme', which had been discontinued in August 1941, in the wake of 'Aktion 14f13', to be resumed in the lawless space of the concentration camps across the Reich. In many camps experiments were carried out into different methods of killing: in Buchenwald the SS installed a piece of equipment that delivered a shot to the back of the neck, in Mauthausen 'death baths' were introduced, in Dachau prisoners were made victims of large-scale medical experiments – and in Auschwitz the guards busied themselves with the cyanide gas Zyklon B.

The poison gas was stored in airtight sealed metal

tins, and was initially deployed from July 1941 in the battle on vermin, to disinfect housing and clothes. The manufacturer was the Deutsche Gesellschaft für Schädlingsbekämpfung (Degesch) (German Pest Control Company) in Frankfurt am Main, a subsidiary company of IG Farben. The poison was delivered by the Hamburg firm Tesch und Stabenow, whose employees, equipped with gas masks, initially undertook the fumigations, but were later trained as SS medical orderlies. At the end of August or the beginning of September 1941, the exact time cannot be precisely identified, Zyklon B was used at first experimentally, but soon regularly, to murder prisoners. From a temperature of about 26°C the cyanide granules turn into gas on contact with air, and are deadly even in small quantities.

The first victims were prisoners of war from the Soviet Union, and also sick and weak prisoners of other categories, including Jews from forced-labour camps in East Upper Silesia. Around 5 September 1941 the first mass killings took place in Auschwitz, when some 900 Soviet prisoners of war and sick prisoners of other categories were murdered in the cells in the basement of the punishment block (block 11). They also included members of the punishment squad, among them many Poles, who had to pay for the escape of a prisoner. The division of labour in the removal and use of the corpses was soon perfected. Prisoners had to drag the corpses from the cellar to the courtyard of the punishment block, undress them, heave them on to trolleys and bring them to freshly dug mass graves. Partly to keep events secret from the other prisoners, and also because the removal of the corpses from the cellar was hard work, in 1941 the murder operations were transferred to the crematorium of the parent camp, which had been put into action in 1940, and which was later called the 'old crematorium', or 'crematorium I'. The mortuary was turned into a gas chamber: the doors were sealed and openings made in the ceiling for Zyklon B to be poured in. By December 1942 the crematorium served as a place of extermination, and by July 1943 it was used to incinerate the bodies of the murdered prisoners. The parent camp was closed off every time a killing operation was in progress; noisy engines ran and horns blared to drown out the cries of the dying.

Birkenau

In Birkenau, formerly Brzezinka, about 2 kilometres away from the parent camp, the construction of a camp of gigantic dimensions began in autumn 1941. For his expansive settlement plans Himmler wanted to intern tens of thousands of Soviet prisoners of war here and engage them in forced labour. There were plans for a 'prisoner of war camp' for 50,000 inmates, which could later be enlarged first to 150,000, and later to 200,000 prisoners.

Birkenau, before the German invasion a place of around 3,800 inhabitants, many of them Jews, was at this point deserted. Since the beginning of the war the Jews had been brought to ghettos in the surrounding area, and the Poles had also been deported in the wake of the settlement policy in the spring of 1941. Contrary to what Rudolf Höss said in his notebook and statements towards the end of the war, the day on which the decision was taken was not 1 March 1941, when Himmler visited Auschwitz for the first time. The order for the construction of the new camp was in fact given on 26 September 1941.

Early October 1941 saw the arrival of SS-Hauptsturmführer Karl Bischoff, the head of the hastily founded central building administration of the Waffen-SS and the police in Auschwitz, whose chief task was to coordinate the building work. The site originally selected was not Birkenau, but a tract of land in the Auschwitz district of Zasole, adjacent to the parent camp. It was Höss who drew the planners' attention to Birkenau while walking around the site; on 4 October 1941 the location was agreed upon and work began a few days later.

The conceptual similarity with the Majdanek camp near Lublin, built at the same time (the decision to build was made the day before the Birkenau decision), is striking: Majdanek, not far from the major settlement project of Zamość in the General Government, was built as a prisoner of war camp, and served at first as a source of labour.

With the construction of Birkenau administrative innovations came into force in Auschwitz: for the arriving Soviet prisoners of war the SS issued a new set of prisoner numbers, but also retained in parallel the numbering system introduced in 1940, so that there were two series of numbers in operation; a third was added in 1942, for re-education prisoners. The Soviet prisoners of war had to have their prisoner numbers tattooed on their left breast with a metal stamp fitted with needles. Jews who arrived from mid-1942 in mass transports from the whole of Europe had the number tattooed on their forearms with a single needle. From spring 1943 this regulation applied to prisoners of all categories (with the exception of Reich Germans and re-education prisoners), both for the new arrivals and for those already registered. Only in the case of those deported to Auschwitz in large numbers, and Jews who were generally murdered upon arrival, did the SS forgo tattoos. In other camps prisoners wore their numbers on metal tabs around their necks, or on a chain or cord around their wrist; tattooing was the practice only in Auschwitz. When, from September 1943, babies born in the camp – supposedly around 700 in all – were not killed immediately, but registered as 'new arrivals', they too, unless they were Reich German children, received tattoos on their thighs or buttocks.

Living conditions in Birkenau were even more catastrophic than they were in the parent camp. On the boggy ground stood brick-built barracks, without paved floors, heating or electric light. The sleeping-places were three-tiered bunks of 4 square metres. The barracks were designed for 180 people, but the SS squeezed in more than 700. Most of the prisoners were housed in windowless wooden stables, sheds cobbled together out of thin wooden boards with two little hatches. The stables consisted of fifty-two horse-boxes; at least 400 prisoners slept on three-tiered wooden bunks that had been brought in. There were at first no sanitary arrangements, either in the brick buildings or in the wooden

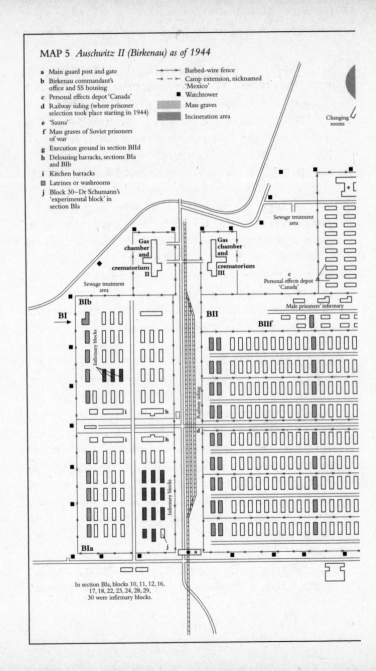

MAP 5 *Auschwitz II (Birkenau) as of 1944*

a Main guard post and gate
b Birkenau commandant's office and SS housing
c Personal effects depot 'Canada'
d Railway siding (where prisoner selection took place starting in 1944)
e 'Sauna'
f Mass graves of Soviet prisoners of war
g Execution ground in section BIId
h Delousing barracks, sections BIa and BIb
i Kitchen barracks
▣ Latrines or washrooms
j Block 30 – Dr Schumann's 'experimental block' in section BIa

✕—✕— Barbed-wire fence
✕—✕— Camp extension, nicknamed 'Mexico'
■ Watchtower
▨ Mass graves
▨ Incineration area

Changing rooms

Sewage treatment area

e

Gas chamber and crematorium II

Gas chamber and crematorium III

Sewage treatment area

c Personal effects depot 'Canada'

Male prisoners' infirmary

BIb

BI

Infirmary blocks

BII

BIIf

i **h**

i **h** **d**

Railway siding

Infirmary blocks

BIa **j** **a**

In section BIa, blocks 10, 11, 12, 16, 17, 18, 22, 23, 24, 28, 29, 30 were infirmary blocks.

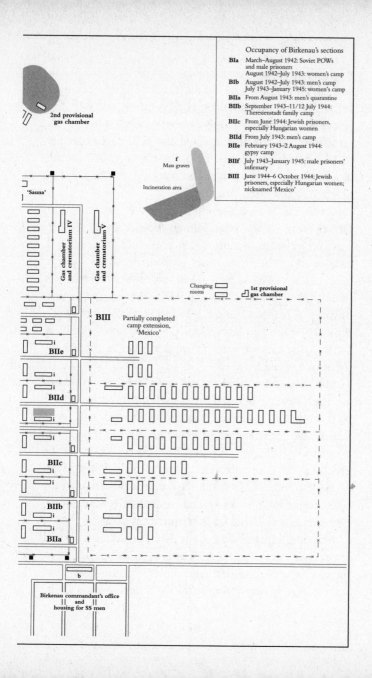

2nd provisional
gas chamber

f
Mass graves

Incineration area

'Sauna'

Gas chamber
and crematorium IV

Gas chamber
and crematorium V

Changing
rooms

1st provisional
gas chamber

BIII   Partially completed
camp extension,
'Mexico'

BIIe

i

i

BIId

i

i

BIIc

BIIb

i

BIIa

b

Birkenau commandant's office
and
housing for SS men

Occupancy of Birkenau's sections

BIa   March–August 1942: Soviet POWs
and male prisoners
August 1942–July 1943: women's camp

BIb   August 1942–July 1943: men's camp
July 1943–January 1945: women's camp

BIIa   From August 1943: men's quarantine

BIIb   September 1943–11/12 July 1944:
Theresienstadt family camp

BIIc   From June 1944: Jewish prisoners,
especially Hungarian women

BIId   From July 1943: men's camp

BIIe   February 1943–2 August 1944:
gypsy camp

BIIf   July 1943–January 1945: male prisoners'
infirmary

BIII   June 1944–6 October 1944: Jewish
prisoners, especially Hungarian women;
nicknamed 'Mexico'

stables. The place was crawling with vermin; a constant lack of water made the situation worse, leading to epidemics such as spotted fever and typhus. It was only the epidemics, which not only sent the death-rates in the camp soaring but also affected the SS estate, that led the camp administration to build washing and latrine blocks in 1943, and sanitary installations were also fitted in some of the brick buildings.

About 10,000 Soviet soldiers arrived in Auschwitz in October 1941. They were initially housed in a separate part of the parent camp, which was reached through a gate bearing the inscription 'Russian prisoner of war labour camp'. The supply of Soviet prisoners of war was initially thought to be inexhaustible. For economic and nutritional reasons, hundreds of thousands of them were thus abandoned to starvation. Of a total of 5.7 million Soviet prisoners of war, 3.3 million died, 2 million of them by February 1942.

After just a month fewer than half of the Soviet soldiers were left alive. In February 1942 their numbers had fallen to 2,000, and in March 1942 the remaining 945 were transferred to Birkenau. In May 1942, 186 of those prisoners were still alive. When it became clear that Soviet prisoners of war were not going to be supplying the massive numbers of workers expected, Birkenau camp was transformed, in a sequence of decisions that cannot be reconstructed, into an extermination camp.

After the mass deaths of the Soviet soldiers it would seem that Jews were to be brought in as a work-force for the expansive settlement projects 'in the East', and sent to Auschwitz–Birkenau in their tens of thousands.

In January 1942 Himmler announced the arrival of 150,000 Jews, a third of them women. The plan was not realized in its entirety, but the first mass transports of women occurred in March. Ten blocks in the parent camp, separated off by a wall, served as the women's camp; at first it fell under the administration of the Ravensbrück camp, where the women had come from. When they were transferred to Birkenau in mid-August 1942, a new women's camp was set up in sections BIa and BIb (all the areas of the camp had shorthand names consisting of letters and Roman numerals). Some 13,000 women moved into the barracks, by which time around 5,000 had already perished. With the female prisoners the first female warders arrived at the SS site of Auschwitz. Commandant Höss, who did not think the female guards were entirely suitable, ordered an SS man to each position, so that all the main camp, report and command positions in the women's camp were always filled twice over.

The Birkenau camp remained at first a sub-camp of the much smaller parent camp; in November 1943 it was made an autonomous camp in the wake of the administrative restructuring after Höss's transfer.

6

The extermination centre

The equipment and technique of mass murder

Mass extermination in Auschwitz–Birkenau occurred in phases, according to technical installations and logistical plans. There is much to suggest that Höss was mistaken when he said in hearings after the end of the war that Himmler had ordered him to Berlin 'in the summer of 1941', and given him the task of murdering the European Jews. For the systematic killing of the Jews in the camp did not begin before 1942. Auschwitz–Birkenau became the centre of mass extermination only in 1943, when Bełżec was already abandoned; the murders in Sobibór and Treblinka had been stopped after the attempted uprisings of 14 August and 1 October 1943, and the deportations to Majdanek, where the remaining 8,000 or so Jews were shot early in November 1943, had also been brought to an end.

It cannot be clearly established whether the first temporary gas chamber in Birkenau, where the mass killings began, was used at the start of the year or only from the spring of 1942. It was installed in the house of a resettled farmer, which the SS called the 'red house' because of its unwhitewashed brickwork, and later also 'bunker 1'.

Not far from it a second temporary gas chamber was set up in the (whitewashed) 'white house', also known as 'bunker 2', which was probably used for the first time in May 1942.

The trains of deportees at first stopped about 2.5 kilometres away from the two houses, level with the Birkenau camp, by a siding of the Auschwitz goods station that ended in an open field. Here the people were unloaded, after journeys that had often lasted for days and weeks, which they had survived in cattle trucks, crammed together, hungry, thirsty and in appalling sanitary conditions, beaten and shouted at by the SS. Separated according to sex, they marched in columns past SS doctors and other functionaries. Anyone who was not selected as fit for work had to walk on foot to the two bunkers; at night trucks went there. Under the pretext that they were to be showered, they were led inside naked. 'Bunker 1' had the capacity for about 800 people, 'bunker 2' for 1,200. When the rooms were full, the air-tight doors were closed, and SS fumigators poured in Zyklon B through openings in the side walls. SS doctors supervised the murder operations, but had to be especially sure that SS men were not poisoned themselves, something that happened before an odoriferous substance was mixed with the poison to prevent that kind of accident.

The corpses of the murdered prisoners were taken to the crematorium of the parent camp, or were thrown into nearby mass graves and scattered with lime. In September 1942 Sonderkommando 1005, an SS special squad led by SS-Standartenführer Paul Blobel, began to dig up the corpses and, to erase the traces, have them burned by the prisoners in the open air on wooden grilles, and sometimes in ditches. Blobel had organized mass shootings as *Sonderkommandoführer* ('special squad leader') of Einsatzgruppe C at Kiev and Poltava. From June 1942 he led the burning of bodies, known as 'exhumation operations', throughout the whole of the conquered East, and also in Chelmno extermination camp, where Höss had inquired into the method used in mid-September 1942. Within about three months Blobel had about 100,000 corpses burned in Auschwitz–Birkenau, and the ashes tipped into the Vistula and Soła.

The murder operations in the two bunkers lasted until spring 1943. Then the houses were abandoned and the corpse-burning trenches levelled. While 'bunker 1' was demolished, 'bunker 2' was left standing – and in May it was used again in the wake of the mass murder of the Hungarian Jews. The SS now wanted new, larger complexes. From autumn 1941 onwards plans were made to build crematorium II in the parent camp. The plan failed initially, but from July 1942 the new crematorium in Birkenau came into operation. It was built by the firm Huta Hoch- und Tiefbau AG (Huta Structural and Foundation Engineering) in Kattowitz; the Silesian industrial construction company Lenz & Co. AG had turned the job down because of a shortage of labour. The company Topf und Söhne from Erfurt was given the job of installing the cremation ovens and other equipment, including electric hoists for the transportation of corpses from the gas chambers to the crematoria, and 'gas-testing equipment' to measure any remaining cyanide. But the second crematorium was not enough. In August 1942 the decision was made to build additional 'crematoria'; by now the term had come to mean 'sites of mass killing'.

Crematorium III was built along the layout of crematorium II; they lay symmetrically to the right and left of the main road through the camp. Crematoria IV and V were arranged in a similar way; because of the tall trees near by the SS referred to them as the 'forest crematoria'. All four constructions were some distance away from the prisoners' barracks; they were disguised by electrified barbed wire, trees and shrubs, and SS men armed with machine-guns sealed off the area.

Construction of the killing installations lasted far into 1943, partly because of bad weather, but also because Topf und Söhne had to develop special models – technical innovations that they had patented in October 1942. The criminal purpose of the equipment was not concealed from the engineers, in particular Kurt Prüfer, who developed the plans and supervised the work. But the task was eventually completed, and solutions for technical problems were energetically sought. Prüfer suggested, for example, the installation of a heating system in the gas chamber of crematorium II, to speed up the effect of Zyklon B in the winter. The SS later returned to this idea, and placed portable coal stoves in the gas chambers.

Crematorium IV was the first to be completed, and was handed over to the SS on 22 March 1943. Crematorium II followed on 31 March, crematorium V on 4 April, and on 24 June, last of all, crematorium III.

Including the 'old crematorium' (crematorium I), in the parent camp, which was closed down in July 1943, the crematoria, according to the calculations of Topf und Söhne, reached a cremation capacity of 4,756 corpses a day.

With a capacity of 1,440 corpses a day each, crematoria II and III were the largest. The incineration rooms in both buildings were on the ground floor, while in the cellar there were a changing room, a gas chamber and a *Leichenkeller* (mortuary). On the steps leading to the changing room there hung a panel, in German, French, Greek and Hungarian, showing the arrivals the way to the 'bathroom' and the 'disinfection room'. Benches and numbered clothes-hooks in the changing room suggested that the prisoners would be returning to their personal effects. Here there were also panels bearing such mottoes as 'One louse – your death' and 'Through cleanliness to freedom'. On the door to the gas chamber it said 'Bath and disinfection room', and from the ceiling hung sieves mounted on pieces of wood, to look like shower heads. Sometimes the SS handed out soap and towels before they shut the gas chambers, each holding up to 2,000 people. The Zyklon B entered the room through four special installations: they looked like pillars surrounded by metal grilles and protruded from the roof. They were hollow inside, and from outside they looked like chimneys. The SS men poured in the poison from the roof, and sealed the openings with concrete plates.

The airtight door to the gas chamber was locked with an iron bolt that could be screwed tight. At eye level there was a peephole consisting of a double pane of glass, about a centimetre thick, protected against the blows of the suffocating prisoners by a metal grid. Through this opening SS men watched them dying, which could last twenty minutes and more. When the victims were dead, ventilators sucked out the poison gas; in crematoria IV and V, in which there was no ventilation system, the doors leading outside were opened.

The mortuary, which was adjacent to the gas chamber in crematoria II and III, was used for collecting the clothes, spectacles, prostheses and hair of the murdered people. The corpses were hoisted on an elevator from the cellar up into the incineration room, which was equipped with five ovens for every three mortuaries. On the same floor in crematorium II there was a dissection room, and in crematorium III a room where gold teeth were melted down. A washroom next to the incineration room was used in both of these buildings (unlike crematoria IV and V) for shootings, which regularly occurred when transports with fewer than 200 people arrived; the victims were murdered in groups of five with shots fired at close range to the nape of the neck.

In crematoria IV and V the changing room and the gas chamber, which consisted of three or four smaller rooms and also held about 2,000 people, were not in the cellar but, like the incineration system, on the ground floor. Here too there were benches and numbered clothes-hooks in the changing room. Only the shower-head fittings in the gas chamber were missing. In the outside walls, as in the 'red house' and the 'white house', there were window-sized openings, closable with metal flaps, through which the Zyklon B was thrown into the gas chambers. The process was the same as in the other extermination camps, and here too SS doctors observed the mass murder. The ashes of the incinerated corpses from all four crematoria were poured into nearby trenches, loaded on to trucks from there, and scattered around the surrounding rivers and ponds or spread as fertilizer on the fields.

As the SS burned far more corpses than they had technically planned for – rather than two, as many as five in half an hour – the incineration ovens and chimneys soon suffered massive damage. The crematoria repeatedly failed through overheating, for example in summer 1944, when the corpses were burned in the open air again, and the specialists had to be called in from Erfurt to repair the equipment.

The removal of the corpses was carried out by prisoners from the *Sonderkommando* ('special squad'). It consisted predominantly of Jewish camp inmates of various nationalities, as well as some non-Jews and Soviet prisoners of war. There were about eight of them in April 1942, soon rising to 200; at the beginning of 1944 about 400; and finally, in July 1944, and during the last high phase of mass murder, when the squad had to work in both day and night shifts, almost 900. They loaded the luggage of the new arrivals off the trains at the ramp, accompanied them to the crematorium building to undress and pulled their corpses out of the gas chamber; they had to break the gold teeth out of the jaws of the dead, pull their rings from their fingers and cut off the women's long hair. Then they carted the corpses on hoists or in tubs to the incineration room, burned them, and dug mass graves and incineration trenches. If the corpses were burned in trenches, which took hours, supervised and spurred on by the SS, they had to check the fire and, to air it, stir the burning bodies with steel hooks; unburned bones were smashed to dust.

The German Reich itself profited from the corpses: gold from teeth was melted down and handed to the Reichsbank in ingots. Human hair was spun into thread and turned into felt for the war industry, and presumably it was also used in the manufacture of mattresses and ropes; among the clients, who paid 50 pfennigs per kilo, were the Bremer Wollkämmerei (Bremen Wool Carding Company) and the Alex Zink felt factory near Nuremberg. Ash was used not only as fertilizer, but also as a filling material in the building of roads and paths and insulation for camp buildings. The SS sold human bone-meal to a fertilizer company in Strzemieszyce.

As the extermination was to remain secret, the *Sonderkommando* was housed in strict isolation from the other prisoners in special barracks, initially in the punishment block of the parent camp, and later in Birkenau men's camp. In mid-1944 the prisoners were transferred to the crematoria grounds, where they were housed in the attic. Work in the *Sonderkommando* extended life expectancy by only a few weeks, eight months being the longest known. After that the prisoners were generally shot. When new transports arrived, a new *Sonderkommando* was formed as well, and assigned in groups to the crematoria. No one volunteered for this task, and many committed suicide shortly afterwards. Only a few of the 2,000 or so prisoners who had to serve in the *Sonderkommando*

survived, and later bore witness to the crimes; some
secret notes and diaries by various chroniclers have also
survived.

Early in 1943 and again in 1944 there were plans to
build another, even bigger extermination and incineration plant in Auschwitz, crematorium VI, but it was
never made. By the time the mass transports arrived
from Hungary in May 1944, after a construction period
of barely a year the long-planned siding into Birkenau
camp was ready, just next to crematoria II and III, the
one that the SS dubbed the 'Jewish ramp'.

Deportees from all over Europe were allowed to bring
between 30 and 50 kilos of luggage to the camp, which
was taken from them immediately after their arrival.
Up to 2,000 prisoners worked in two shifts as a clearing squad to collect and sort the bundles of food, household goods, clothes and medicine; furniture and carpets
also ended up in the camp, along with currency, clocks
and jewellery. The personal effects were stored in thirty
barracks surrounded with barbed wire, which were
built following the construction of camp section BIIg
at the end of 1943. In camp jargon the storage grounds
were called 'Canada' – after the country which, in the
eyes of the Polish prisoners who had coined the term,
was immeasurably wealthy. Working in 'Canada' was
seen as a privilege, and objects from the stores, which
were purloined despite extremely severe punishments,
became a valuable currency in the camp.

This plunder was state property: the Reichsbank
received money and precious metals, and textiles, shoes
and household goods went to ethnic German settlers; IG

Farben, the Todt Organisation, the *Reichsjugendführung* ('Reich Youth Leadership') and various concentration camps also benefited. Luftwaffe pilots, U-boat crews and bombed-out residents of Berlin received (the less valuable) wristwatches. Several hundred fully laden railway trucks left the camp in 1943. Every month gold, jewellery and currency ended up in at least two lead-lined boxes, each of which is supposed to have weighed over a ton, in trucks headed for Berlin.

Vast amounts of money and valuables vanished into the pockets of the SS men of Auschwitz, who helped themselves unscrupulously despite the threat of the death penalty. If suspicions were aroused, the men covered for one another, which is why discoveries like that of the commission led by SS-Sturmbannführer Konrad Morgen in July 1943 were quietly forgotten.

The civilian population could not help but see that the warehouses of the camp were full of desirable treasures. It speaks volumes about the perception of events in Auschwitz that families from the SS settlement, and also civilians from outside, applied to the camp administration to find out whether the goods might be for sale, or perhaps even to be had for free.

The murder of the Jews

At the end of March 1942 the first mass transports organized by the RSHA arrived in Auschwitz–Birkenau. On the night of 25 March 1,000 arrived; two days later about 800 Jewish women from Slovakia; on 30 March there followed more than 1,100 Jewish men and women of various nationalities from French internment camps. The Jews, whose labour force had been expressly requested by the RSHA, were not murdered immediately, but registered and received into the camp. Systematic extermination operations began in May 1942 – the victims were Jews from Upper Silesia, Slovakia, France, Belgium and the Netherlands – and from July 1942 they became the rule.

There were presumably pragmatic reasons why mass transports from western Europe to Auschwitz–Birkenau were introduced from summer 1942, because after the Wehrmacht's spring offensive transport was blocked both to Majdanek and to the Operation Reinhard camps. To all appearances, Auschwitz–Birkenau served as a place of last resort. The technology of murder was now expanded, and the killing capacity increased.

On 17 and 18 July 1942, Himmler came on a two-day inspection of the camp. He visited the agricultural estate, and granted permission for some building projects, but at the centre of his visit was the demonstration of a mass killing. He had the different stages presented to him, using a transport from the Netherlands: from prisoner selection to killing in the gas chamber of 'bunker 2', and the deployment of the *Sonderkommando*. At the evening reception in the house of the Gauleiter ('district leader') of Upper Silesia, Fritz Bracht, the Reichsführer-SS is said to have expressed great satisfaction. Before he visited the building site in Monowitz with senior IG Farben managers the following day, he promoted camp commandant Höss to SS-Obersturmbannführer. Shortly afterwards Himmler determined that the General Government, with the exception of a few collection camps, was to be 'Jew-free' by the end of the year.

In Auschwitz, the number of mass transports of Jews from the whole of Europe rose month by month. If Jews had formed only a small proportion of the prisoners at the start of the extermination operations, from now on they formed the largest group. Arriving transports were no longer registered and numbered, but murdered directly after the selection process. The transports from western Europe were followed by Jews from countries that were German allies, and whose governments had consented to the deportation: Romania, Croatia, Finland and Norway, and later Bulgaria, Italy and Hungary. Other countries and regions later joined in, including Yugoslavia, Denmark, Greece and the southern part of France at the end of 1942 and the start of 1943.

The first German Jews on a transport organized by the RSHA arrived from Vienna in mid-July 1942. German Jews from Beuthen had already been transported to Auschwitz in February 1942, probably in connection with regional anti-Jewish measures in Upper Silesia. In November and December 1942 the first mass transports from the Old Reich followed from Berlin. After the order was given in 1942 that the concentration camps in the Old Reich were to be made *judenrein* ('Jew-clean'), the 2,000 Jews imprisoned there were brought to Auschwitz–Birkenau. Because of a drastic labour shortage, the regime revised this measure in March 1944; Jewish prisoners then returned to the camps to work for the munitions industry, chiefly underground (especially in

Mittelbau-Dora, which belonged to Buchenwald, and Kaufering, a sub-camp complex outside Dachau).

A transit camp to mass extermination in Auschwitz–Birkenau was the ghetto of Theresienstadt (Terezin). Here, old Jews from inside the Reich, Jewish soldiers from the First World War and their families, as well as *Mischlinge* ('half-castes'), who were considered to be Jews after the Nuremberg laws, as well as Jewish spouses from dissolved 'mixed marriages' and Jews from the protectorate of Bohemia and Moravia were imprisoned. The deportations from Theresienstadt began on 8 September 1943. About 18,000 men and women were brought to the so-called 'family camp', the separated-off BIIb section of Birkenau. What was unusual – at least temporarily – was their treatment: the Jews of Theresienstadt were neither separated according to sex nor subjected to the selection process, and they did not have to give up their luggage; they were allowed to keep their civilian clothes, and the children were allowed to stay with the adults. They received all kinds of privileges, and only some of them were assigned to the work units. There were a school and a kindergarten, housed in a barracks that they were allowed to paint with fairytale scenes.

Like the Theresienstadt ghetto, the family camp in Birkenau served the propaganda purposes of the regime. Its goal was to rebut the information that was spreading around the world of the murder of the Jews. The privileges granted the Jews from Theresienstadt lasted for about six months, and then the SS disbanded the family camp in two stages; almost all the inmates were murdered in March and July 1944, and about 3,000 were transferred to another camp.

In the summer of 1944 the mass extermination reached a final peak. Up to 10,000 Hungarian Jews arrived each day for selection at the newly built 'Jews' ramp'. Between 15 May and 9 July about 438,000 people appeared there; about 15 per cent were taken into the camp, and all the others were killed immediately. Their murder was one of the biggest extermination operations of all. Hungary had refused deportations for a long time, despite massive pressure from the Germans. But after the country was militarily occupied, and a satrap government had been formed, the exterminations began there too – led by Adolf Eichmann, the organizer of the Jewish transports in the RSHA. Coordination of the mass murder was also performed at a high level within the camp itself: Rudolf Höss returned to Auschwitz for this special task. Within a few weeks Höss had fulfilled his mission; awarded the War Merit Cross first and second class, he left the camp on 29 July 1944 to go back to Berlin.

The difficult transport conditions did not prevent the RSHA from deporting Jews from Rhodes, Corfu, Crete and other Greek islands to Auschwitz–Birkenau. From 60,000 to 70,000 Jews from Łódź, the last ghetto to be destroyed in occupied Poland, came to the camp in September and October 1944, as did Jews from Slovakia. On 30 October 1944 a train carrying around 2,000 Jews from Theresienstadt was the last Jewish mass transport, and presumably also the last to undergo 'selection'.

Other groups of victims

Sinti and Roma, the so-called gypsies, were persecuted for racial reasons in the Old Reich even before the beginning of the war, and locked up in concentration camps. In December 1942 Himmler ordered that they be detained for the duration of the war; shortly afterwards Auschwitz–Birkenau became the central collection point. On 26 February 1943 the first transport arrived from the Old Reich; in stages, by 1944, a total of around 22,600 gypsies were brought to Auschwitz–Birkenau, about half of them children and young people.

About 1,700 gypsies were murdered shortly after their arrival, supposedly as they were suspected to have spotted fever, and the others were registered with 'Z' series prisoner numbers. The SS introduced series of numbers with symbols and letters only in the wake of the mass receptions. 'A' and 'B' designated Jews. The gypsies were, like the Jews of Theresienstadt, crammed together in families in a separate section of the camp (BIIe), which was also called a 'family camp', and for a while they had similar privileges: they kept their civilian clothes, did not have to cut their hair short, were allowed to keep their luggage, and for the children a barracks building was transformed into a kindergarten. The gypsies were not, unlike other prisoners, obliged to do forced industrial labour, but were instead assigned to heavy digging and building work, and were employed, for example, in the building of the ramp and the laying of the tracks in Birkenau. Living conditions in the gypsy camp were disastrous, and within a short space of time about 7,000 men, women and children died, most of them from typhus, but many, especially the youngest, died of the malnourishment disease noma (gangrenous stomatitis), which was unknown in other parts of the camp.

In May 1944 Himmler ordered the murder of the gypsies; about 3,000 had by then been transferred to other camps. Many now fell victim to deliberate killing by phenol injections to the heart, a method that the doctors and medical orderlies called *abspritzen* ('to inject to death'). On 2 August 1944 this section of the camp was dissolved, and the last gypsies were killed at night in crematorium V.

Another major group of victims was made up of non-Jewish Poles. Especially among the *Polizeihäftlinge* ('police prisoners'), a separate category under the supervision of the political department, their numbers were very large. They were arrested for violation of the Polish Special Punishment Directive, and locked in basement cells in the punishment block of the parent camp. Police prisoners came before the police court, which was regularly presided over in the punishment block by the head of the Kattowitz Gestapo (until September 1943 SS-Sturmbannführer Rudolf Mildner, and then SS-Obersturmbannführer Johannes Thümmler). Sessions of the court, which turned the Auschwitz camp into a legal centre, were regularly held at intervals of four to six weeks from January 1943. In many instances, more than 100 rulings were passed after summary proceedings, nearly all of them ending with a death sentence, which was immediately carried out in the courtyard of the punishment block, by the 'Black Wall'. Among those condemned by the police court were young people, children and old people, and also Soviet prisoners of war. Camp Commandant Liebehenschel had the Black Wall demolished in December 1943, although that did not mean the end of the executions, which were carried on in crematorium IV by shooting in the back of the neck.

Doctors in Auschwitz

Many National Socialist concentration camps served as sites for 'medical research'. Auschwitz was the centre of the human experiments that the regime encouraged in the service of studies important to the war effort. Specialists in many areas of medicine came to Auschwitz, including noted scientists. They set up examination rooms, laboratories and operating theatres; they mutilated, murdered and dissected the prisoners. And those who survived the experiments generally died of the after-effects.

The gynaecologist Carl Clauberg was the senior doctor at a women's hospital in Königshütte in Upper Silesia. From late 1942, in some rooms on the upper storey of block 10 of the parent camp, he used hundreds of women to study methods of mass sterilization and artificial fertilization. The camp doctor Eduard Wirths and his brother, a gynaecologist from Hamburg, also carried out experiments on women. SS-Sturmbannführer Horst Schumann ran the institutes of Grafeneck and Sonnenstein near Pirna, where mentally and physically handicapped people were murdered as part of the so-called 'euthanasia' programme. He was in the Auschwitz camp in July 1941, as part of 'Aktion 14f13', where he led a medical commission and organized the removal of more than 570 'invalids', chronically ill and elderly prisoners, to the killing institution of Sonnenstein. Schumann came to the camp as a doctor in 1942 and spent as much as one and a half years experimenting with X-rays to render men and women infertile. Johann Paul Kremer, Professor of Anatomy and Human Genetic Theory at the University of Münster, carried out research on weakened prisoners from August to November 1942, in a series of studies into hunger, examining the consequences of food withdrawal for the human organism. Also interested in the connection between hunger and life expectancy was SS-Obersturmführer Hans Münch, a physician and late in 1943 Bruno Weber's deputy at the Hygiene Institute of the Waffen-SS in Auschwitz. The institute, which employed chemists, biologists and doctors, was created between 1942 and 1943 as part of the Berlin SS-Sanitätsamt ('SS Medical Board'). Most of the so-called research concentrated on infections such as spotted fever, malaria and syphilis. Experiments were performed on dead and living prisoners: body-parts from murdered prisoners were used for bacteriological studies, and for haematological investigations living prisoners were employed, many of whom bled to death.

In May 1943 SS-Hauptsturmführer Josef Mengele came to Auschwitz. The 32-year-old was qualified in medicine and anthropology (he had been made a doctor of philosophy for his work in the latter field). He had been fighting, with the SS Division 'Viking', on the Eastern front, probably until the beginning of that year. He was wounded and ordered back to Berlin, before once more being transferred to the East. The assistant to Otmar Freiherr von Verschuer, the director of the Kaiser Wilhelm Anthropological Institute in Berlin-Dahlem, Mengele clearly found ideal conditions for his lecturer's dissertation in Auschwitz. Mengele's specialist field was genetics, above all research into twins, as well as with the physiology and pathology of dwarfism. Using around 1,000–1,500 pairs of twins, he experimented in the laboratories set up for him in the gypsy family camp and the prisoner infirmary buildings of Birkenau. His preferred subjects were children. He sent internal organs, eyes – especially those with differently coloured irises – as well as the heads of gypsy children suffering from noma as anatomical preparations to the Kaiser Wilhelm Institute.

SS-Hauptsturmführer August Hirt, director of the Anatomical Institute at the Reich University in Strasbourg, devised anthropological studies – lethal to their subjects – to prove the superior value of the 'Aryan' race in Auschwitz: Hirt arranged for dozens of prisoners, almost all of them Jews, to be measured in the summer of 1943, and then brought to Natzweiler–Struthof concentration camp in Alsace, where they were killed. He made their skeletons part of his large anatomical collection. In December 1944 the Hamburg doctor Kurt Heissmeyer had Jewish children brought to the Neuengamme camp for what were referred to as investigations into tuberculosis; at the end of his studies they were dead, Heissmeyer having had them hanged in April 1945 in an attempt to cover up his human experiments. Other doctors, including Friedrich Entress, Helmuth Vetter and Eduard Wirths, infected prisoners with spotted fever to test vaccines, or tried out newly developed medicines, particularly on behalf of IG Farben. The Wehrmacht used Auschwitz prisoners for experiments with toxic substances, which produced tumours and inflammations. The doctors were supposed to be using them to examine ways of detecting those, like soldiers at the front, who were faking illness.

7

The final phase

Auschwitz and the Allies

An extremely fast information network that had been built up by local and regional clandestine organizations in cooperation with the secret resistance group in the camp made sympathizers in the area around Auschwitz very important. Using messengers and radio transmitters, they managed to send messages about the crimes as well as lists of the names of SS men to Cracow and London. The Polish government in exile, which had reported on the brutality in Auschwitz since November 1941 in the English-language *Polish Fortnightly Review*, was able to publish reports on gassing experiments in the camp as early as 21 July 1942.

The first horrific news had been reaching the international public via the BBC in London since autumn 1943. By then at the very latest the Allies, the Vatican and some neutral states were informed of the crimes. Through Gerhart Riegner, a representative of the World Jewish Congress in Geneva, who had received reliable information through connections in Breslau, the Americans and the British had already been alerted by telegram in August 1942. Riegner's information came from an industrialist who had attended the reception for Himmler in the *Gauleiter*'s private house, where it would appear that people had spoken openly about the mass murder. The telegram warned that all Jews from the countries occupied and controlled by Germany were to be concentrated in the East and eradicated there. 'Methods, including cyanide, under discussion,' it said. But the authorities gave no credence to Riegner's telegram.

Reports about the systematic murder of the Jews also reached the public directly from the camp. They were based on the accounts of Alfred Wetzler and Rudolf Vrba (Walter Rosenberg), two Jewish prisoners from Slovakia who had managed to escape to their homeland on 7 April 1944 with the help of the resistance movement within the camp. They urgently warned representatives of the Slovakian Jewish Council about the liquidation of the transports from Theresienstadt in their 'family camp', and about the imminent killing of the Hungarian Jews. They gave a precise account of the course of the extermination process, described the way the crematoria worked, and provided information about the organization of the camp, the everyday life of the prisoners, and the interconnection between the SS and industrial companies; they gave dates, departure points, numbers of prisoners and numbers of deaths. From Slovakia via Hungary and Switzerland their report reached the World Jewish Congress, a complicated and protracted journey. But the paper was not used to warn and save the Hungarian Jews, not even after it had been completed and updated by Czesław Mordowicz and Arnošt Rosin, two Slovakian prisoners who had also managed to escape from Auschwitz on 27 May 1944. The dossier or abbreviated versions of it reached Allied positions in mid-June 1944, and before long had travelled as far as neutral Sweden and the Vatican. The BBC broadcast some details, and the Swiss press published articles, as did American newspapers and radio stations. In mid-1944, in the countries opposing Germany in the war and in neutral states, more and more was published about Auschwitz in the press.

Despite the interest of the public, the political effect of such descriptions was slight. The Allies took no action against the mass extermination. Appeals and demands by the Polish government in exile (from as early as August 1943) and Jewish organizations in Great Britain and the USA fell on deaf ears; the killing institutions were not bombed.

After American reconnaissance flights the Allies had their first aerial photographs of Auschwitz in April 1944, and from the end of June 1944 the pictures were so detailed that it was possible to make out the extermination sites, and even see the ramp and people walking towards the crematoria – presumably prisoners on their way to the gas chambers. Since the construction of an air force base in Foggia in Italy early in 1944 Auschwitz was no longer outside the range of the Allied bombers. The strategic and technical conditions for bombing crematoria and railway lines were thus in place. But the Allies paid no apparent attention to the murders happening there. The American War Department resolutely rejected the idea of any operation because the camp was not seen as a military installation. And what was more, according to the British, an attack could not be carried out for lack of air power. But Allied squadrons regularly flew over Birkenau camp, when the nearby synthetic oil refineries were bombed between July and November 1944. On five occasions the IG Farben plant had been the target of Allied attacks: on 20 August, 13 September, and 18 and 26 December 1944, and on 19 January 1945. A stray bomb fell not far from the parent camp, damaged a siding (not used for death transports) and killed forty prisoners and fifteen SS men. But gas chambers and tracks leading to Birkenau were left undamaged.

The Sonderkommando uprising

No other group in the camp was so closely confronted with mass murder as the prisoners in the *Sonderkommando*. Although their 'work' led to desensitization, apathy and despair, *Sonderkommando* prisoners had, in summer or autumn 1943, formed a circle of their own, including many who had fought with the French Resistance and the communist underground in Poland. Their goal was to capture weapons, destroy the extermination centres and organize a break-out. They managed to establish contact with the general resistance movement in the camp and the leaders of Combat Group Auschwitz. But conflicts of interest emerged, because the military council of the Combat Group hesitated, wanting to risk an uprising only after careful preparation. For that reason the *Sonderkommando* independently pushed ahead with its plans for an uprising that was to spread from the crematoria to the camp and unleash a mass escape among the prisoners. However, because of the arrival of large numbers of SS troops, the planned rebellion had to be postponed. An SS prisoner selection finally prompted the uprising: after an attempted escape the SS had murdered 200 members of the *Sonderkommando* with cyanide in a storage room used for personal effects. Three hundred further prisoners were to follow, and it was the responsibility of the *Sonderkommandos* of crematoria IV and V to make the selections. When, on the morning of 7 October 1944, the SS announced that those selected were to be transferred to another camp the same day, the same message as had been given to prisoners murdered in the past, the uprising broke out: just before half-past one in the afternoon prisoners attacked approaching SS men in crematorium IV with stones, axes and iron bars, set the building on fire with smuggled hand-grenades and fled. The smoke alarmed the prisoners in the other crematoria. The SS set up machineguns in crematorium IV and fired into the crowd of prisoners; those who were not hit immediately were forced into crematorium V, which faced crematorium IV. The rebellion spread to crematorium II, where the prisoners managed to part the barbed wire and flee, at least temporarily. Beyond the 'outer cordon' some made it to the adjacent forests, and others to the fish-breeding plants and agricultural estates in Rajsko, where they were able to arm themselves and attack the SS. Some of them hid in a barn, where they were locked in and burned alive.

The uprising was not quelled until the evening; crematorium III alone was left untouched, because during the fighting SS men surrounded the building and locked the prisoners in. The losses among their own ranks show that the SS had not expected violent resistance: three camp guards were dead and at least twelve injured; the *Sonderkommando* suffered about 425 casualties. The SS continued with their murders for about three days. The victims included Ester Wajcblum, Regina Safirsztajn, Ala Gertner and Roza Robota, the Jewish women who had smuggled explosives from their work-place in the Weichsel Union Metallwerke into the camp under their clothes, and given them to the *Sonderkommando* to make hand-grenades. After a week of torture they were hanged in the parent camp on 6 January 1945.

No prisoner managed to escape during the uprising, but the rebellion was not in vain: crematorium IV was in ruins, and even before that the *Sonderkommando* prisoners had managed to take photographs and smuggle the film out of the camp with the help of Combat Group Auschwitz. Early in September 1944 it reached the Polish resistance movement in Cracow. Two pictures show *Sonderkommando* prisoners standing by burning corpses in the courtyard of crematorium V, and in a third only the tall tops of the trees can be seen around the killing installation; another shows women having to undress in the open air before going to the gas chamber.

The dissolution of the camp and the death march

In July 1944 Soviet troops marched into Galicia and south Poland through German lines, liberated the camp of Majdanek, hastily evacuated by the SS guards, crossed the Vistula and were just 200 kilometres away from Auschwitz. The systematic dissolution of the camp began. Thousands of prisoners and huge amounts of personal effects from the warehouses, as well as building material and equipment, were transported in trains and lorries to the Old Reich during the first clearance phase between summer 1944 and January 1945. About half of the 155,000 or so prisoners who were held captive in summer 1944, the period of the highest level of occupation, most of them Poles and Russians, were brought to concentration camps in the west by the autumn: Buchenwald, Flossenbürg, Ravensbrück, Dachau, Mauthausen, Gross-Rosen, Bergen–Belsen, Natzweiler, Sachsenhausen and Neuengamme. Many prisoners who had survived Auschwitz died now from hunger, epidemics and the deadly conditions they had to live in. In March 1945 in the already overcrowded camp of Bergen–Belsen some 18,000 deaths were recorded. The victims included Anne Frank and her sister Margot, who had been deported in September 1944 with the last transport from Westerbork in Holland, and brought to Bergen–Belsen with an evacuation transport late in October 1944.

Nothing changed in the daily routine in Auschwitz, even while the camp was being broken up. Prisoners still had to turn up for forced labour, new buildings were under way in the parent camp, development work was beginning in the sub-camps, and even a series of new external camps was coming into being. In Birkenau work had started on the construction of a new section, called BIII, or in prisoner slang 'Mexico'. The grounds were so enormous that it would nearly have doubled the size of the camp, a clue to the regime's further megalomaniac plans for murder. But 'Mexico' was never completed, because all building work stopped in October 1944.

On an order from Himmler to cease extermination operations across the Reich all gassing systems were shut down in November 1944; the previous month 40,000 people had been murdered. The *Sonderkommando* had to dismantle the killing installations and remove all traces of the crimes. The corpse-burning trenches had to be cleared and levelled, and hollows in the camp grounds which had been filled with the ashes and bones of the murdered prisoners were to be emptied, covered with turf and planted over. Crematorium I in the parent camp was turned into an air raid bunker. The chimney and the holes in the ceiling through which the Zyklon B was thrown in disappeared, the ovens were dismantled, and the passageway between the gas chamber and the incineration room was closed. The SS had crematorium IV, badly damaged during the *Sonderkommando* uprising, pulled down. Usable parts of the other equipment, including the incineration ovens of crematoria II and III, were transported to other camps, presumably to Gross-Rosen, possibly to Mauthausen, where the ventilation equipment from the gas chambers also ended up.

In January 1945 the Red Army encircled German troops after a surprise offensive near Cracow, took over the Upper Silesian industrial belt almost undamaged, and pushed as far as Brieg and Steinau on the Oder below Breslau. Gauleiter Fritz Bracht, who as Reich Defence Commissar responsible for the region had for a long time refused to abandon his policy of holding out until the very end, ordered the evacuation of the district capital, Kattowitz, and extended the clearance order to the whole region. Detailed guidelines established at the end of December 1944 governed the evacuation of the Auschwitz camp. The aim was to send the prisoners westwards in columns, first on foot and later by rail, so that they could still be used for forced labour in the Old Reich. Two routes were established for the parent camp and Birkenau: one via Pless and Rybnik, the other via Tychy and Gleiwitz; prisoners from the sub-camps had to march via Beuthen, Tost and Oppeln.

On 17 January 1945, with the evacuation of some 58,000 prisoners, the second and final phase of the clearing of the camp complex began; about 20,000 of them came from the parent camp and Birkenau, and all the rest from Monowitz and the sub-camps. A very few were taken away by train in goods trucks, but most were marched on foot in the winter cold along the roads of Upper and Lower Silesia. Thousands died on the death march. Anyone who weakened or fell, anyone who tried to rest or flee, was shot by the SS. In some areas, despite the fact that it was strictly forbidden and subject to severe punishment, some civilians handed bread to the people drifting by, or were prepared to take in refugees; in areas inhabited predominantly by Germans such offers of help were not forthcoming.

After several days' march the prisoners were sent to Gleiwitz and Wodzisław Śląski in open goods trucks. Many froze or starved to death on the way, and in the regions of northern Moravia, northern Bohemia and annexed Austria, through which the trains passed on the way to the Old Reich, corpses were left lying along the tracks. All in all, about 15,000 prisoners died during the evacuation. Around 43,000 arrived in the camps in the west, where as 'new arrivals' they were once more at the bottom of the hierarchy of prisoners. Anyone who survived until the spring of 1945, when the SS dissolved the camps inside the Reich as well, was sent on yet another death march. In May 1945 the SS loaded about 7,000 prisoners from Neuengamme on to two German naval vessels, including prisoners from Auschwitz. The Allies, who knew nothing of the human freight, sank the *Cap Arcona* and the *Thielbeck* in the bay of Lübeck. There were no survivors.

By the middle of January 1945 the Lager-SS in Auschwitz was feverishly trying to remove the written evidence of mass murder. Files, death certificates, lists and other papers from the camp administration were burned in big rubbish incinerators, boilers and open bonfires in the camp grounds. The dossiers of the political department and the central building administration were hastily packed away and taken to Gross-Rosen and other camps. The X-ray machine that had been used until the spring of 1944 for Horst Schumann's medical experiments was removed. His colleague Mengele closed down the experimental laboratories and corpse dissection rooms only when he had no 'human material' left at his disposal. With the departing prisoners, he left Auschwitz on 17 January 1945, and took the written documentation of his murders with him.

In the chaos of the dissolution of the camp the hundred or so remaining *Sonderkommando* prisoners were able inconspicuously to join the marching columns. The SS, whose plan it was to murder the last immediate witnesses of mass murder, did not manage to find the men among the evacuated prisoners. They were able to leave the camp, and almost all of them survived the war.

On 20 and 21 January 1945 the SS removed their sentries from the watchtowers; small units still patrolled the grounds. It is not known whether the order to clear the camp and murder the remaining prisoners was given at this time. But within a week, 300 Jews and a further 400 prisoners of different categories were killed in various sub-camps.

What remained of crematoria II and III was blown up on 20 January 1945; components of the killing equipment, ready for transport, were later discovered by the liberators on a building site near the camp. Before they themselves left Auschwitz, the SS guards set fire to the personal effects storeroom 'Canada'; the camp was still burning days later, and only six out of thirty barracks were left standing. Crematorium V, where executions by shooting in the back of the neck were still taking place, and where corpses were burned, remained ready for operation until the final days; only during the night of

25–6 January 1945 was the last extermination installation blown up.

A day and a few hours later, on the afternoon of 27 January 1945, a Saturday, soldiers of the 60th Army of the First Ukrainian Front liberated Auschwitz and its sub-camps. They found at least 600 corpses. In the parent camp, in Birkenau and in Monowitz some 7,000 prisoners were still alive, about 5,800 of them in Birkenau, about 800 in the prisoners' infirmary building in Monowitz, and 500 in the smaller sub-camps. Many were already so weak that they were barely aware of the event they had so long yearned for.

In the warehouses the liberators found about 370,000 men's suits, 837,000 women's coats and dresses, huge amounts of children's clothing, about 44,000 pairs of shoes, 14,000 carpets, and prostheses, toothbrushes, household goods and, in the former leather factory near the parent camp, 7.7 tonnes of human hair packed ready for transport. They calculated that it must have come from about 140,000 women.

8

The town and the camp after liberation

The end of the 'model town'

The IG Farben plant was almost ready for production when it was hurriedly cleared ahead of the advancing Soviet troops. What remained behind was the greatest ruined investment of the German Reich in the Second World War. German women and children were evacuated from Auschwitz from the end of October 1944. Administrative officials, IG Farben managers and civilians also left the town on special trains in mid-January 1945. In the chaos of the last days of the war, racial order had still been preserved: the fleeing Reich Germans had precedence over the concentration camp prisoners on the streets and tracks, and the marching columns of the prisoners of war and forced labourers.

The 'model town' of Auschwitz met a pitiful end: in September 1945 about 7,300 people still lived in the town, which now belonged to the newly founded Polish state and was once more known as Oświęcim. Poles made up 5,000 of the residents; the rest included 68 Ukrainians, 33 French people, 8 Russians and 4 Czechs. There were also 186 Jews – and about 2,000 ethnic Germans. The latter were probably the Polish inhabitants who had joined the

German *Volksliste* during the occupation, either voluntarily or under pressure. There were no other Germans.

The machines and high-pressure synthesizing plants of the IG Farben factory were swiftly dismantled by the Soviets and moved to Kemerovo in western Siberia, where a coal-hydration complex was being built. In Oświęcim one of the biggest plastics factories in Poland emerged out of the remaining plants. Of the former German residents who returned to the Old Reich little is known. It seems likely that many of them quickly got back on their feet, like the architect Hans Stosberg, who rebuilt the destroyed city of Hanover after the war.

The careers of many surviving Auschwitz prisoners were marked by illness and severe mental problems. Some of them were the only survivors of their sizeable families. The sense of guilt at being alive, a deep sense of alienation in the face of a social environment that was unable to imagine or to grasp what they had been through, and the signs of trauma that still appeared years after the liberation marked them and continue to mark succeeding generations.

Military hospital, prisoner of war camp, memorial

With the support of helpers from the surrounding area the Soviet liberators set up a military field hospital in the former parent camp. In the barracks of Birkenau a field hospital was set up by the Polish Red Cross, which moved after a few weeks to the brick buildings in the parent camp. In day and night shifts doctors, nurses and carers tended to the survivors of the camp, most of them Jews, including around 200 children. In the weeks that followed the liberation many died of the consequences of imprisonment in the camp, perhaps because their emaciated bodies had been unable to cope with too sudden a rush of food. In many cases the psychological effects were even more serious than the physical ones. In some the announcement of bathtime prompted a panic reaction, as did the sight of needles, and some survivors would not stop hiding bread under their pillows. After about three to four months, however, many were capable of returning to their homelands with transport organized by the military authorities, or on their own initiative.

In April 1945 camps of the Soviet political secret police, the NKVD (People's Commissariat of Internal Affairs), were set up in the former prisoners' blocks in the parent camp and in Birkenau women's camp. Interned in them were Wehrmacht soldiers, civilians from the surrounding area of Upper Silesia, members of the *Volkssturm* ('people's storm', i.e. militia) and Germans from Bohemia who had been captured by the Americans and handed over to the Soviets; they also included ethnic German Poles. But few details are known, and it is unclear, for example, how many prisoners were held here before being transferred to the Soviet Union. The NKVD camp in the parent camp was dissolved at the end of 1945, and the prisoner of war camp in Birkenau is thought to have been dissolved in May 1946.

Early in 1946 the Soviet authorities placed most of the former camp grounds under the auspices of the political administration. In March 1946 prisoners' organizations and the Polish authorities came up with an initiative to set up a museum in the camp grounds. The following year the project became a reality. With the law of 2 July 1947 the state memorial of Auschwitz–Birkenau came into being. Exhibitions were organized, the archive and the library were built up and rebuilding work was undertaken (for example, in the old crematorium). The exhumation of corpses continued until the end of the fifties. In the former Monowitz camp, which remained a factory, a memorial stone recalls the victims of forced labour. The former camp complex, which has been a protected memorial since the foundation of the memorial site, was made a World Cultural Heritage Site by UNESCO in 1979. Today the memorial attracts half a million visitors from all over the world every year.

The number of victims

From the very beginning the investigative commissions – a Soviet commission took up the work in February 1945, a Polish one in April – have examined the question of the number of victims. After the compound had been examined, the ruins of the extermination systems studied and the statements of some 200 surviving prisoners recorded, the Soviets made a public statement on 8 May 1945. Four million people, according to the communiqué published in the newspaper *Krasnaja Zvezda*, were murdered in Auschwitz. It did not mention how many of those were Jews. The quoted figure was based on the estimated incineration capacity of the crematoria, and was quickly broadcast around the world. The Nuremberg Tribunal trying the 'major war criminals' picked up the figure, as did the newly founded Supreme National Court in Poland, and textbooks and encyclopaedias quoted the figure of 4 million dead. But since the SS had almost completely destroyed the precise deportation plans at the end of the war, former prisoners had given various figures and Höss spoke of 3 million dead – according to him, 2.5 million were killed with gas, and half a million died of hunger and epidemics – different figures were soon in circulation. The figures ranged from less than a million to over 6 million. Today, drawing from far more accurate information, it is certain that at least 1.1 million, and possibly up to 1.5 million people were murdered in the Auschwitz camp complex. That corresponds to about 20–25 per cent of all the Jews killed in the Second World War.

The question of the number of Auschwitz victims is further complicated by the fact that the Lager-SS had a small number of prisoners registered and numbered. No more than about 400,000 prisoners of various nationalities received a prisoner number and about half of those were Jews. The so-called 'death books' kept by the camp registry office, which was set up in 1941, contain around 69,000 names, because records were not kept about those killed in the mass extermination operations. Anyone who was selected immediately after arrival as 'unfit for work', or who had been transported to the camp for execution (including Soviet prisoners of war, those condemned by the camp court and prisoners from other camps) was killed without having been registered.

It can be proven that the National Socialists murdered 5–6 million Jews during the Second World War. The overall figure varies between 5.3 and 6.1 million – a discrepancy produced by the fact that even today it is impossible to arrive at precise figures for the murdered Soviet Jews. The bulk of the victims, about 3 million, were murdered in the extermination camps, about 1.3 million died in mass shootings and about a million in ghettos and concentration camps; almost 700,000 were killed in mobile gas-lorries, and around 800,000 died of hunger and disease in the ghettos.

About 90 per cent of those murdered in Auschwitz, a total of around 960,000, were Jews. Of those, 438,000 came from Hungary, about 300,000 from Poland, 69,000 from France, some 60,000 from the Netherlands, 55,000 from Greece, 46,000 from Bohemia and Moravia, about 27,000 from Slovakia, 25,000 from Belgium, around 23,000 from the Old Reich, 10,000 from Croatia, about 6,000 from both Italy and Belorussia, 1,600 from Austria and some 700 from Norway. Others killed included 70,000–75,000 non-Jewish Poles, 21,000 so-called gypsies, 15,000 Soviet prisoners of war and 10,000–15,000 members of other nations, among them Czechs, Russians, Belorussians, Ukrainians, Yugoslavians, French, Austrians and Germans. About 200,000 further prisoners died from hunger, disease and inhuman working conditions.

These calculations are based on a series of sources that have been found in the interim, which make it possible to determine the number of victims in a much more sophisticated fashion than was possible immediately after the liberation. These include fragments of copies of the accession lists of deported Jews, which provide dates and places of departure of the extermination transports. Also preserved are forms from the company Tesch und Stabenow concerning the delivery of Zyklon B, as well as three reports by the Lager-SS to Berlin authorities, indicating how many members of a transport were destined for labour deployment and how many were to be sent to the gas chambers. Also important are the hand-written notes of *Sonderkommando* prisoners, which were discovered in the camp grounds in 1952, 1962 and 1980, as well as sketches and drawings by survivors. Also of central importance is the official correspondence from the countries of origin of the deportees. These document the preparation of the transports, as well as detailed train timetables with figures and precise lists of the names of Jews. Architectural blueprints for the crematoria have been available since the opening of the eastern European archives in the early nineties.

There have been intense discussions in the field of contemporary history about the possibility that the number of those murdered could in fact be smaller than statements made after the war might have indicated. The first academic study that critically engaged with the question of numbers, and discussed sources as well as methods of calculation, was an essay by the French researcher and former Auschwitz inmate Georges Wellers, published in 1983. Independently, the Polish historian Franciszek Piper reached similar conclusions in the book that he published in the early nineties; while Wellers reached a figure of 1.4 million victims, Piper was able to make a more precise estimate, based on a wider range of sources, of the number of Polish prisoners killed. Piper concluded that at least 1.1 million had been murdered, but did not rule out a maximum figure of 1.5 million. The Auschwitz–Birkenau memorial, which had long kept to the figure of 4 million victims, accepted Piper's figures in the late nineties. The debate about numbers is not a relativization of the crimes, but rather confirms the central importance of Auschwitz–Birkenau in the National Socialist extermination policy.

9

Auschwitz before the courts

Trials in Poland

After the end of the war several hundred members of the Auschwitz SS appeared before various courts in Poland, more than in any other country, but still only a fraction of the 7,000 men and women who had served in the camp. According to estimates, at least 6,300 former SS members were still alive at the end of the war. Between 1946 and 1949 about 1,000 of them had been tracked down, most of them in the American zone of occupied Germany. They had been extradited to Poland in line with the Moscow Declaration of October 1943, in which the foreign ministers of the Soviet Union, Great Britain and the United States had announced that they would hand German war criminals over to the countries on whose territories their crimes had been committed. Between 1946 and 1953 the Polish judiciary brought accusations against at least 673 people, 21 of them women. Most of the proceedings were held in district, voivodeship and special criminal courts in Cracow and Wadowice.

Two trials were also held by the highest Polish judicial authority, the Supreme National Court, founded in Warsaw in February 1946, whose sole task was to bring German war criminals to justice. Here the highest-ranking SS officials in Auschwitz were put on trial: Commandant Rudolf Höss and – along with thirty-nine other members of the Lager-SS – Commandant Arthur Liebehenschel.

After the end of the war Höss had gone into hiding as an agricultural worker by the name of Franz Lang, on a farm near Flensburg. British officers had soon arrested him on suspicion of belonging to the German navy, but his true identity remained unrecognized. It was not until March 1946 that the British discovered who he really was and arrested him again. At the end of May 1946 Höss was handed over to Poland. First he spoke as a witness for the defence before the International Tribunal in Nuremberg in the trial of Ernst Kaltenbrunner, Heydrich's successor as head of the RSHA, who was later condemned to death. Before being handed over, Höss was heard as a witness on several further occasions, including the preparation for the subsequent Nuremberg trials of the SS Economic Administration Head Office and IG Farben.

While in custody in Cracow, Höss wrote an account of his life, several hundred pages long, which he entitled *My Psyche. Development, Life and Experience*. Like a book-keeper, he sets out the details of mass extermination, and yet, as in the Allied hearings, he makes many errors concerning dates and contexts. His memoirs, which were published in Polish in 1956 and two years later in the original German, document his obsession with his duties as organizer of the 'Final Solution', but also testify both to a lack of awareness of wrongdoing, and a remarkable level of sentimental narcissism.

The Warsaw trial of Höss began in the presence of many foreign observers and journalists on 11 March 1947; at the beginning of April Judge Alfred Eimer passed the death sentence. In the grounds of the parent camp, next to the SS camp administration block, and not far from the villa where he formerly lived as commandant, Höss was hanged on 16 April 1947.

The Cracow Supreme Court trial of forty Lager-SS members, the largest that was ever held in relation to Auschwitz, began on 25 November 1947. The highest-ranking official among the accused was the former commandant Arthur Liebehenschel. The accused followed a common strategy: they shifted responsibility to the executed Höss. For twenty-three of them the trial ended with a death sentence in any case, announced six days after the end of the trial on 22 December 1947. Among those executed were Liebehenschel, Lagerführer ('camp leader') Hans Aumeier, the head of the political department Maximilian Grabner, and Maria Mandel, camp leader of the women's camp. Seven of the accused were condemned to life imprisonment, including two female warders. The court passed nine sentences of imprisonment, six of them for more than fifteen years. Two of the accused who had been sentenced to death, SS camp doctor Johann Paul Kremer and Johann Arthur Breitwieser, later had their sentences commuted to life imprisonment, and were transferred to the Federal Republic of Germany in the late fifties. There was also one acquittal: SS doctor Hans Münch, formerly deputy-director of the

SS Hygiene Institute and responsible for studies into hunger among the camp inmates, went unpunished because prisoners had spoken up in his favour.

Allied judgements and early judicial practice in the Federal Republic of Germany

Allied military judges did not hold an actual trial on the subject of Auschwitz. None the less, in line with the Potsdam Agreement, many SS guards were brought before the courts in Allied concentration camp trials, because towards the end of the war many of them had been transferred back inside the Reich and taken prisoner there. In the Bergen–Belsen trial in British-occupied Lüneburg, the first trial by a military tribunal of German Nazi criminals, hearings were specifically devoted to the Auschwitz crimes from September until November 1945. Josef Kramer, who before he was appointed camp commandant of Bergen–Belsen held the same position in Auschwitz–Birkenau, as well as Franz Hössler, camp leader in the parent camp and in Birkenau women's camp, and the two Auschwitz warders Elisabeth Volkenrath and Irma Grese were sentenced to death by hanging.

In the Dachau trial that began in November 1945 an American military tribunal passed a death sentence on a number of Auschwitz SS men, including Vinzenz Schöttl, camp leader in Monowitz, Otto Moll, director of the crematoria in Birkenau, and the SS camp physician Friedrich Entress. In the Natzweiler trial a French

military court sentenced to death Friedrich Hartjenstein, commandant of Auschwitz–Birkenau, along with
Heinrich Schwarz, commandant of Monowitz. In the
Mauthausen, Buchenwald and Ravensbrück trial Auschwitz SS men also appeared before the court. In the
Nuremberg trial of the 'major war criminals' the camp
itself was not explicitly the subject of proceedings.

In March 1946 the directors of the Hamburg company
Tesch und Stabenow, which had delivered Zyklon B to
Auschwitz, appeared before a British military court. The
owner Bruno Tesch and his business manager were
sentenced to death and executed. The technicians working with the extermination installation attracted the
particular attention of the occupying forces. At the end
of May 1945 the engineer of the crematoria, Kurt Prüfer,
was arrested by the Americans. The same night Ludwig
Topf, co-owner of the company Topf und Söhne, committed suicide. His brother, Ernst Wolfgang, presented
himself to the American authorities, but for unknown
reasons was left in peace and founded a new business
in Wiesbaden in 1947: a company making ovens for
crematoria. The engineer Prüfer, freed by the Americans,
was arrested by the Soviets in Erfurt in 1946 and sentenced to twenty-five years in a penal camp. He died
in 1952.

The pressure to prosecute eased considerably when
the investigation of Nazi criminals became a matter for
the judicial authorities in the newly founded Federal
Republic. The idea of exculpating those who were seri-
ously incriminated entered into the federal legal system.
The young Federal Republic's attitude to the past meant

that a speedy end to investigations as well as an amnesty and social integration for the incriminated parties was to be expected. Polish applications to have the perpetrators handed over were increasingly seen as a national humiliation, and from 1950 they went unanswered.

Doctors and business managers who had actively promoted the selection of prisoners and their mass murder in Auschwitz escaped with mild sentences in the new federal state, or escaped criminal prosecution completely. Gerhard Peters, for example, general director of Degesch, which produced Zyklon B, was acquitted after two court appearances in Frankfurt am Main in 1955.

In the fifties doctors no longer needed to worry about accusations, and no one who had carried out killings in the context of the 'euthanasia' programme was found guilty of murder, because 'base motives', the precondition for such a judgement, could not be assumed. The mass murderer Horst Schumann, who had opened a medical practice under his own name in Gladbeck in Westphalia, moved to the Sudan in the early fifties, presumably having been tipped off by the authorities. Nigeria and Libya were his next stopping-points, before he entered the state health service in Ghana. Schumann was tried in 1970 in the Federal Republic, after he had been handed over four years previously. But the trial had to be interrupted on grounds of Schumann's ill health, and in July 1972 he was freed from captivity; until his death in 1983 he lived freely in Frankfurt am Main.

Johann Paul Kremer, who was brought before the

court again in Münster in 1960 after being released from Polish imprisonment, did lose his academic title, but despite being sentenced to ten years' imprisonment he was able to go home a free man because the court ruled that he had served his term in prison in Poland. Carl Clauberg had been condemned to twenty-five years' imprisonment in the Soviet Union in 1948, but after being granted a 'special pardon' he returned to the Federal Republic in 1955, where he made no secret of his human experiments in Auschwitz and even boasted about his method of mass sterilization. In response to public pressure Clauberg was arrested a few weeks after his return, and put on trial two years later. In 1957 Clauberg died in custody in Kiel. Josef Mengele had been released unrecognized as a prisoner of war of the Americans, and first went into hiding near his Swabian home town of Günzburg, where his family, who supported him, ran a flourishing farm machinery factory. By the time his identity came to light in the late fifties he had already moved to South America, where, like many Nazi criminals, he did not have to fear extradition. Thirty years after his escape from Germany Mengele lost his life in a swimming accident in Brazil in 1979.

The management of IG Farben also profited from the political considerations of the post-war period. Ten of the twenty-four leading officials who had to answer to the courts in the Nuremberg IG Farben trial were acquitted on 30 July 1948 after a year's proceedings, while the rest were given custodial sentences of between one and a half and eight years. If the US authorities pursued 'Case VI' only half-heartedly, this was in part due to the world political situation, because, as the Cold War developed, German industrialists came to be seen as indispensable for the economic and military security of western Europe. The major perpetrators from IG Farben were given custodial sentences – Otto Ambros and Walther Dürrfeld received the maximum sentence of eight years – but were quickly pardoned after the foundation of the Federal Republic. Released by January 1951 into the euphoric atmosphere of the 'Economic Miracle', there was nothing to prevent them from rising back to senior positions in industry: Carl Krauch, Fritz ter Meer, Walther Dürrfeld and Heinrich Bütefisch, all of them once holding directorial roles in the IG Farben works in Auschwitz, were important players in the reconstruction of the Federal Republic's chemicals industry; Ambros was immediately given management positions in several large companies.

In January 1952, in the Frankfurt seat of the former company headquarters, IG Farben went into liquidation; four months later twelve subsidiary companies were formed out of the large combine. After legal action was brought by Norbert Wollheim, a former Jewish prisoner in the Monowitz camp, the shareholders of the dissolved company undertook to pay 30 million marks in compensation to the victims of forced labour. From now on 6,000 former Jewish prisoners received payments of between 2,500 and 5,000 marks; a tenth of the overall sum went to non-Jewish camp inmates. These payments, made specially with a view to improving the company's image, had a favourable impact on values on the stock exchange: after the compensation agreement the share value of 'IG Farbenindustrie in Liquidation' immediately rose by about 10 per cent.

The Frankfurt Auschwitz trial and other proceedings

The Frankfurt Auschwitz trial was brought about both by chance and by the commitment of a very few people. The attorney-general of the Federal German state of Hesse, Fritz Bauer, who had initiated many proceedings against Nazi criminals, had received from a journalist documents owned by a surviving Auschwitz prisoner, containing lists of names of members of the SS who had 'shot escaping prisoners'. Henceforth Bauer became the driving force behind the criminal investigations that he brought before the regional court in Frankfurt am Main in June 1959, with the agreement of the Federal Court of Justice.

No less strikingly, at around the same time, in the town of Schwäbisch-Hall, investigations by the Stuttgart public prosecutors had begun into one of the most brutal torturers of the political department in Auschwitz. In March 1958 Wilhelm Boger, inventor of the torture device known as the 'Boger Swing', was reported by a former prisoner for mass murder. Six months passed before a warrant for Boger's arrest was issued, because the man who had reported him, who was himself in prison for perjury, was considered to be a notorious liar, and the International Auschwitz Committee supporting him was decried as communist. But once the investigations were under way, and the cooperation of

Hermann Langbein, the secretary-general of the International Auschwitz Committee, had been secured, arrests followed in quick succession. Richard Baer, the last commandant of Auschwitz, who had been living unchallenged under a false name as a forestry worker near Hamburg, was arrested late in 1960. But Baer died in custody before the trial began; following him in terms of SS rank was Robert Mulka, the former adjutant to Commandant Höss, who now became the chief defendant. The case 'against Mulka and others' (file 4 Ks 2/63) was opened by the director of the regional court, Hans Hofmeyer, on 20 December 1963 in the Römer city hall in Frankfurt, attracting public attention all around the world; in April 1964 the court moved into the newly built House of Gallus. The trial was witnessed by 20,000 visitors in the course of its twenty-month duration, among them countless school classes; the media reported the case in detail; and in the music-less oratorio *Die Ermittlung* (*The Investigation*), by Peter Weiss, the trial also made it on to the stage.

Public interest was aroused above all by the statements of surviving prisoners, and it was these that gave the Frankfurt trial its particularly striking profile. More than 350 men and women, most of them living abroad and no longer in the best of health, undertook the journey to Frankfurt and endured the nervous strain of facing the former SS thugs and describing features of life in the camp. For many of them it was their first meeting with Germans since the end of the war.

The subject of the trial was not the 'administrative mass murder' (Hannah Arendt) of the bureaucrats and 'desk perpetrators'. Instead, the defendants were accused of a multitude of concretely provable individual crimes. And it was clear that the people before the court were not beasts, which made cosy attribution of guilt in the public discussion all the more difficult. The accused were henchmen and executors of the mass extermination, including seven former SS officers who, unlike the decision-makers at the top of the Nazi regime, and unlike the organizers of the extermination transports in the local public authorities, had directly confronted the victims with violence, the arbitrary use of force and annihilation. Not one of the twenty-two accused showed any sense of guilt, or even any insight into their individual responsibility for the murders (apart from Baer, the SS medical orderly Hans Nierzwicki also escaped trial, for reasons of ill health; in the course of the trial the block leader Heinrich Bischoff died, and the medical orderly Gerhard Neubert was declared incapable of standing trial because of a kidney infection). But none of them, while protesting his personal innocence, denied that a huge amount of killing had been carried out.

The judicial and political climax of the trial was the field inspection of Auschwitz. In the judicial process of the Federal Republic, it was customary in the case of capital crimes to visit the scene of the crime, particularly if no confessions were forthcoming. A court delegation directed by Walter Hotz, the appointed judge and member of the court, travelled to Poland in mid-December 1964. The visit behind the Iron Curtain was a very bold undertaking, particularly since the Federal Republic did not yet have diplomatic relations with

Poland, and there could be no question of normalizing relations between the states. The fact that the field inspection could none the less take place in the chilly political climate of the sixties was thanks to the commitment of the lawyer Henry Ormond, the *Nebenklage* advocate (under German law the victims of a crime have a right to influence proceedings; this is called *Nebenklage*, and a lawyer is assigned to facilitate the process), and his Polish colleague Jan Sehn, the head of the Criminological Institute of Cracow University. As a member of the Polish Investigatory Commission in the camp, Sehn had already set criminal investigations in motion immediately after being liberated from the Nazis, and also led the forensic investigations in the two Auschwitz trials by the Supreme Court.

Eleven of twenty-two defence counsels, three public prosecutors and the three *Nebenklage* advocates, a recorder, two judicial officers, a court photographer and an interpreter attended the inspection. The only defendant who decided to return to Auschwitz was the former SS physician Franz Lucas. Between 200 and 300 journalists from all over Europe, the USA and Israel turned the inspection, which began on 14 December 1964 with a minute's silence by the (reconstructed) Black Wall in the parent camp, into a major publicity event. The 2½-day visit was central to the trial. Its significance lay in ascertaining the facts, and in its lasting psychological effects on the participants in the trial. It became apparent that almost all the statements by the former SS men could be contradicted, and conversely that many of the charges could be substantiated. It was clear, for example, that the parent camp had not been too big, as the defendants claimed, for them to know what was happening. The whole of the camp compound could be seen from every watchtower. Through holes in the roof, peep-holes and gaps in the wooden beams over the windows, prisoners could actually observe what was happening, and SS men could be recognized from a distance taking part in the selection process. The field inspection provided something that the trial had not managed to supply in the course of a year: a clear picture of the machinery of extermination.

On 19 and 20 August 1965, after 182 days of hearings, the judgement was reached in the Auschwitz trial. Seventeen defendants were given custodial sentences, and three were acquitted for lack of evidence: Johan Schoberth of the political department, the medical orderly Johann Arthur Breitwieser and the dentist Willi Schatz. Six were given life sentences: Stefan Baretzki, a block leader in Birkenau, Emil Bednarek, Wilhelm Boger of the political department, Franz Hofmann, as 'functionary prisoner' *Kapo* in the punishment unit, the report leader Oswald Kaduk and the medical orderly Josef Klehr. Robert Mulka was given a fourteen-year sentence; in 1968 he was released as unfit to be kept in prison, and died a year later. Hans Stark of the political department was sentenced to ten years; Victor Capesius, who had been in charge of the camp pharmacy, was given nine years; Karl Höcker, adjutant to Commandant Baer, and Willy Frank, head of the dental ward, received seven years; the squad leader Bruno Schlage was given six years; Klaus Dylewski of the political department was sentenced to six years;

the medical orderly Herbert Scherpe four years and six months; Pery Broad of the political department four years; medical orderly Emil Hantl three years and six months; and the camp physician Franz Lucas three years and three months.

Among the accused Lucas had the best chance of acquittal, but the field inspection was – at first – his undoing. Former prisoners had called in after television reports about the visit of the court delegation and levelled such severe accusations at Lucas that, in a sensational confession in March 1965, he had admitted to taking part in prisoner selections, something that he had hitherto vigorously denied. Other untruths came to light, so that Lucas was finally found guilty. But the verdict was overruled in the review proceedings by the Federal Court in February 1969, on the grounds that Lucas's defence, that he had acted under duress, could not be wholly disproved; in autumn 1970 he was finally acquitted by a Frankfurt court.

Admittedly the sentences passed in the Auschwitz trial were considerably lower than the punishments recommended by the state prosecutor's office, and admittedly the reaction among survivors abroad was one of incomprehension and protest, but the trial assumed central importance in the West German treatment of the Nazi past: from a historical and political point of view the Auschwitz trial became the most important attempt to bring a criminal prosecution for the murders. In the Federal Republic the systematic elucidation of the Nazi crimes had begun only towards the end of the fifties. The Auschwitz trial provided the crucial stimulus to political and social engagement with the mass crimes. Historians working in the field of contemporary history within the Federal Republic, who had until then brought out no pertinent study on the subject, drew up pioneering documents, on the initiative of Fritz Bauer, which were read out during the trial and published in 1965 under the title *Anatomie des SS-Staates* (*Anatomy of the SS State*). After the trial interest in the critical examination of Nazi crimes clearly grew, especially among the younger generation.

Legal sanctions against the crimes did not end with the big Auschwitz trial. Four further, less extensive trials were held in Frankfurt am Main, finishing in 1981. In the second trial (December 1965 to September 1966), Josef Erber was sentenced to life imprisonment, Wilhelm Burger to eight years, and Gerhard Neubert, who had been declared unfit to stand in the first trial, to three and a half years' imprisonment. In the third trial (August 1967 to June 1968), of the former 'functionary prisoners' Bernhard Bonitz and Josef Windeck, a second judicial inspection of Auschwitz took place, and two further visits followed. The third trial (December 1973 to February 1976) ended for lack of proof with the acquittal of both defendants, Willi Sawatzki and Alois Frey. In the last trial (1977–81) the accused, Horst Czerwinski, formerly camp leader in the neighbouring camps of Lagischa and Golleschau, was at first declared unfit to stand trial but was later imprisoned for life. His fellow defendant, Josef Schmidt, once a block leader in Lagischa and a guard in the parent camp, was sentenced by the court to eight years' custody.

In March 1966, in East Berlin, the camp physician Horst Fischer, who had been working for decades as a doctor under his own name in Spreenhagen near Frankfurt an der Oder, was put on trial; he was sentenced to death and executed. Czech courts had previously applied death sentences to the medical orderly Adolf Theuer and the warder Sophie Hanel. In Austria, the homeland of many of the Auschwitz SS, their crimes were also brought before the courts, but after the national amnesty of 1957 this occurred only sporadically. Walter Dejaco and Fritz Ertl of the SS central building administration were acquitted in Vienna in March 1972; documents stored in Moscow, showing the two men's signatures on blueprints for the crematoria, were not at the time accessible.

10

The 'Auschwitz lie'

Since the late forties some extreme right-wing apologists have denied the National Socialist mass murder of the Jews and other groups of victims. Organized in networks, they appear worldwide under the self-designated term 'revisionists'. Books, journals and institutions such as the Californian Institute for Historical Review and, most particularly the internet, serve to disseminate their propaganda far beyond their organized and supposedly academic circle. The starting point and core of their theses, which make lofty claims to scientific truth and are passed on through claques of supporters, are aggressive nationalism and racist anti-Semitism. Authentic sources are declared to be forgeries; surviving witnesses are discredited; some documents are given distorted interpretations, others are simply invented. The goal is to sow the seeds of doubt and through wild conjectures to produce contradictions, in order to distort the findings of genuine research. At the centre of revisionist denials, standing for all the mass crimes of the Third Reich, is Auschwitz concentration and extermination camp.

In their shoddy publication of 1947–8 Maurice Bardèche, Paul Rassinier, Robert Faurisson and Austin J. App disputed the existence of gas chambers in Auschwitz and concluded that the high death figures were due not to systematic extermination, but to malnutrition and illness. The question of the number of victims is a central theme of the historical falsifiers. Not only do they trivialize the murders, but, 'running amok against reality' (Martin Broszat), they call the extermination the invention of a Jewish-controlled policy that aims to make the Federal Republic 'vulnerable to blackmail', both politically and financially.

A wave of far-right publications first swept West Germany in the seventies. It began in 1970 with the *Hexen-Einmal-Eins einer Lüge* (*Witch's Multiplication of a Lie*) by Emil Aretz. Three years later came *Die Auschwitzlüge. Ein Erlebnisbericht* (*The Auschwitz Lie. A Report from Experience*) by Thies Christophersen (1973), who had been a member of the SS troops in Auschwitz. Despite being banned, more than 100,000 copies of his book were distributed. *The Hoax of the Twentieth Century* by Arthur R. Butz (1976) was published in German translation in 1977. The pamphlet *Did Six Million Really Die?* by Richard Verrall, alias Richard Harwood, was also translated into German. The Hamburg judge Wilhelm Stäglich, who had been stationed near Auschwitz as a Wehrmacht officer in the Second World War, published *Der Auschwitz-Mythos – Legende oder Wirklichkeit?* (*The Auschwitz Myth – Legend or Reality?*) with the far-right Tübingen company Grabert-Verlag in 1979. The book was impounded across the country the following year, and banned in 1982. Stäglich was removed from state employment after the revocation of his doctorate. Jean-Claude Pressac, who had long been a disciple of Faurisson, also appeared at first as an advocate of 'revisionism', although his investigations into the crematoria of Auschwitz eventually led him to part company with the revisionist circle. Since then Pressac has presented important research into the technology of the extermination systems in Auschwitz, although the total figure of 775,000 deaths that he presents without evidence is not tenable.

In the Federal Republic denial of the Nazi crimes was protected by the right to free speech until 1985, but since then it has been punishable as a crime, first as libel, and since 1994 as incitement to public disorder. The crime is called, pithily if not precisely, the 'Auschwitz lie'.

The revisionists' theses have been made more respectable by professional historians like Hellmut Diwald, Professor of Early Modern History at the University of Erlangen. In his *Geschichte der Deutschen* (*History of the Germans*), published in 1978, he incorporated certain revisionist theses, such as that of 'natural deaths' in Auschwitz. Not so much an apologist as a proponent of resolutely anti-communist views, which were also characteristic of the early revisionists, he appeared in the *Historikerstreit* ('historians' dispute'), as it was called, of the 1980s, when, in a process that was utterly unproductive from the historical point of view, historians questioned the uniqueness of the National Socialist crimes and drew comparisons with the Soviet gulag system.

In the late eighties and early nineties relativization and denial led to the macabre project of attempting to support the 'Auschwitz lie' from a scientific and technical viewpoint. In 1988 Fred R. Leuchter, an American builder of execution equipment, published a report alleging that samples of stone from the crematoria in Auschwitz–Birkenau, which he had taken without permission on a three-day excursion, had shown no traces of hydrocyanic acid. Revisionist circles hailed this as definitive proof of the non-existence of the gas chambers.

The *Leuchter Report* was the result of concentrated activities by the revisionist network around Ernst Zündel, who made a considerable profit in Toronto by issuing racist publications, and was taken to court. To avoid being convicted, Zündel had commissioned Leuchter, the self-appointed engineer, to write the expert report, and paid him for it. The neo-Nazi publicist and publisher Udo Walendy commissioned a German translation of the report, and the foreword was written by Robert Faurisson. Germar Rudolf, in the *Rudolf-Gutachten* (*Rudolf Documents*) confirmed Leuchter's findings.

Finally the historian Ernst Nolte joined in the discussion of the *Leuchter Report*. Nolte did not mention the 'Auschwitz lie' as such, but he did make public statements in which he spoke respectfully of Leuchter's report, and stressed his supposedly scientific approach.

The British writer David Irving, who had written apologias for Hitler and acted as a legal expert witness for Ernst Zündel, took the same line. Since writing the foreword to the English edition of the *Leuchter Report*, Irving had become the figurehead of the international Holocaust deniers. Irving has been forbidden to travel to Germany since the nineties. The libel case that Irving brought before the High Court in London against the American historian Deborah Lipstadt and her publishers,

Penguin Books, ended in failure. Irving was proved to have wilfully misinterpreted the evidence for the mass extermination in Auschwitz. Of crucial importance to the trial were the expert witnesses called by the defendants to throw down the gauntlet to Irving. In a 700-page document Robert Jan van Pelt, a Toronto cultural historian, assembled all available pieces of evidence concerning the extent, the duration and the technology of the murder operations in Auschwitz. The London trial, which was given similar importance in the British press to the Nuremberg trials of the 'major war criminals' and the Eichmann trial in Jerusalem, ended in April 2000 in the first and July 2001 in the second instance, with the dismissal of the libel claim. Since the trial it has been permissible to speak in public of Auschwitz-denier Irving as a falsifier of history, an anti-Semite and a racist.

Published sources and selected eye-witness accounts

Adler, Hans Günter, Hermann Langbein and Ella Lingens-Reiner (eds.), *Auschwitz, Zeugnisse und Berichte*, Hamburg, 1994 (first published Cologne, 1962)

Bezwiska, Jadwiga and Danuta Czech (eds.), *KL Auschwitz Seen by the SS: Höss, Broad, Kremer*, Oświęcim, 1972

Dębski, Jerzy, Sibylle Goldmann, Halina Jastrzbska, Stephanie Kreuzhage and Jan Parcer (eds.), *Sterbebücher von Auschwitz. Fragmente*. Vol. I: Berichte. Vol. 2 and Vol. 3: *Namensverzeichnis A–L, M–Z*, Munich, 1995

Frei, Norbert, Thomas Grotumn, Jan Parcer, Sybille Steinbacher and Bernd C. Wagner (eds.), *Standort- und Kommandanturbefehle des Konzentrationslagers Auschwitz. 1940–1945*, Munich, 2000

Greif, Gideon (ed.), *Wir weinten tränenlos . . . Augenzeugenberichte der jüdischen Sonderkommandos in Auschwitz*, Cologne, 1995

Gutmann, Israel and Bella Guttermann (eds.), *The Auschwitz Album. The Story of a Transport*, Jerusalem, 2002

Hahn, Hans-Jürgen (ed.), *Gesichter der Juden in Auschwitz. Lili Meiers Album*, Berlin, 1995

Höss, Rudolf, *Commandant of Auschwitz. The Autobiography of Rudolf Hoess*, London, 1959 (originally published in Polish, 1956; in German, 1958)

Höss, Rudolf and Steven Paskuly, *Death Dealer: The Memoirs of the SS Kommandant at Auschwitz*, London, 1992

Kielar, Wieslaw, *Anus Mundi. Five Years in Auschwitz*, Frankfurt am Main, 1982 (originally published in Polish, 1972)

Langbein, Hermann, *Menschen in Auschwitz*, Munich, 1999 (first published Vienna, 1972)

Levi, Primo, *If This is a Man*, London, 1962 (originally published in Italian, 1958)

Parcer, Jan (ed.), *Memorial Book: Gypsies at Auschwitz–Birkenau* (2 vols.), Munich, 1993 (Polish and German editions, 1993)

Shelley, Lore (ed.), *Secretaries of Death. Accounts by Former Prisoners Who Worked in the Gestapo of Auschwitz*, New York, 1986

Świebocka, Teresa, Jonathan Webber and Connie Wilsack, *Auschwitz. A History in Photographs*, Bloomington, Indiana, and Warsaw, 1993 (first published Oświęcim, 1990)

Further reading

Allen, Mike Thad, *The Business of Genocide: The SS, Slave Labour, and the Concentration Camps*, Chapel Hill, 2002

Aly, Götz, *Final Solution: Nazi Population Policy and the Murder of the European Jews*, London, 1999 (originally published in German, 1995)

Aly, Götz and Susanne Heim, *Architects of Annihilation: Auschwitz and the Logic of Destruction*, Phoenix, London, 2003 (originally published in German, 1991)

Arad, Yitzhak, *Bełżec, Sobibór, Treblinka. The Operation Reinhard Death Camps*, Bloomington, Indiana, 1987

Auschwitz. Geschichte und Wirklichkeit des Vernichtungslagers, Reinbeck, 1980

Die Auschwitz-Hefte. Texte der polnischen Zeitschrift 'Przeglad Lekarski' über historische, psychische und medizinische Aspekte des Lebens und Sterbens in Auschwitz (2 vols.), Hamburger Institut für Sozialforschung, Hamburg, 1994

Bailer-Galanda, Brigitte, Wolfgang Benz and Wolfgang Neugebauer (eds.), *Die Auschwitz-Leugner. 'Revisionistiche' Geschichtslüge und historische Wahrheit*, Berlin, 1996

Balzer, Friedrich-Martin and Werner Renz (eds.), *Das Urteil im Frankfurter Auschwitz-Prozess (1963–65)*, Bonn, 2004

Bankier, David, *The Germans and the Final Solution: Public Opinion under Nazism*, Oxford, 1996

Bastian, Till, *Auschwitz und die 'Auschwitz-Lüge'. Massenmord und Geschichtsfälschung*, Munich, 1997

Benz, Wolfgang (ed.), *Dimension des Völkermords. Die Zahl der jüdischen Opfer des Nationalsozialismus*, Munich, 1996

Browning, Christopher, *The Origins of the Final Solution: The Evolution of Nazi Jewish Policy September 1939–March 1942*, London, 2004

Buchheim, Hans, Martin Broszat, Hans-Adolf Jacobsen and Helmut Krausnick, *Anatomie des SS-Staates*, Munich, 1999 (first published 1965 (2 vols.))

Czech, Danuta, *The Auschwitz Chronicle*, London, 1990

Długoborski, Waclaw and Franciszek Piper (eds.), *Auschwitz 1940–45: Central Issues in the History of the Camp* (5 vols.), Oświęcim, 2000 (originally published in Polish, 1995)

1. Aleksander Lasik, Franciszek Piper, Piotr Setkiewicz and Irena Strzelecka: *The Establishment and Organization of the Camp*

2. Tadeusz Iwaszko, Helena Kübica, Franciszek Piper, Irena Strzelecka and Andrzej Strzelecki: *The Prisoners: Their Life and Work*

3. Franciszek Piper: *Mass Murder*

4. Henryk Swiebocki: *The Resistance Movement*

5. Danuta Czech, Aleksander Lasik, Stanislaw Klodzinski and Andrzej Strzelecki: *Epilogue*

Dwork, Deborah and Robert Jan van Pelt, *Auschwitz: 1270 to the Present*, New York, 1996

Evans, Richard, *Telling Lies about Hitler: The Holocaust, History and the David Irving Trial*, London, 2002

Frei, Norbert (ed.), *Karrieren im Zwielicht: Hitlers Eliten nach 1945*, Frankfurt am Main, 2002 (first published 2001)

Frei, Norbert, Sybille Steinbacher and Bernd C. Wagner (eds.), *Ausbeutung, Vernichtung, Öffentlichkeit. Neue Studien zur nationalsozialistischen Lagerpolitik*, Munich, 2000

Friedler, Eric, Barbara Siebert and Andreas Kilian, *Zeugen aus der Todeszone. Das jüdische Sonderkommando Auschwitz*, Lüneburg, 2002

Gilbert, Martin, *Auschwitz and the Allies*, London, 2001 (first published 1981)

Gutman, Yisrael (ed.), *Enzyklopädie des Holocaust. Die Verfolgung und Ermordung der europäischen Juden*. German edition edited by Eberhard Jäckel, Peter Longerich and Julius Schoeps, Munich, 1995 (English and Hebrew edition, 1990)

Gutman, Yisrael and Michael Berenbaum (eds.), *Anatomy of the Auschwitz Death Camp*, Bloomington, Indiana, 1994

Gutschow, Niels, *Ordnungswahn. Architekten planen im 'eingedeutschten Osten' 1939–1945*, Berlin, 2001

Guttenplan, D. D., *The Holocaust on Trial*, New York, 2001 (published in German, 2001)

Hefte von Auschwitz, published by the Staatliche Museum Auschwitz–Birkenau, nos. 1–22 and special editions since 1959

Herbert, Ulrich (ed.), *National Socialist Extermination Policies: Contemporary German Perspectives and Controversies*, New York, 2000 (originally published in German, 1998)

Herbert, Ulrich, Karin Orth and Christoph Dieckmann (eds.), *Die nationalsozialistischen Konzentrationslager. Entwicklung und Struktur* (2 vols.), Göttingen, 1998

Hilberg, Raul, *Destruction of the European Jews* (3 vols.), New Haven, 2003 (expanded new edn originally published in German, 1994

Hilberg, Raul, *Sonderzüge nach Auschwitz*, Mainz, 1981

Huener, Jonathan, *Auschwitz, Poland, and the Politics of Commemoration, 1945–1979*, Athens, 2003

Keller, Sven, *Günzburg und der Fall Josef Mengele. Die Heimatstadt und die Jagd nach dem NS-Verbrecher*, Munich, 2003

Klee, Ernst, *Auschwitz, die NS-Medizin und ihre Opfer*, Frankfurt am Main, 1997

Langbein, Hermann, *Der Auschwitz-Prozeß. Eine Dokumentation* (2 vols.), Frankfurt am Main, 1995 (first published 1965)

Lipstadt, Deborah, *Denying the Holocaust: The Growing Assault on Truth and Memory*, Harmondsworth, 1995

Longerich, Peter, *Politik der Vernichtung. Eine Gesamtdarstellung der nationalsozialistischen Judenverfolgung*, Munich, 1998

Mommsen, Hans, *Auschwitz, 17. Juli 1942. Der Weg zur europäischen 'Endlösung der Judenfrage'*, Munich, 2002

Naumann, Bernd, *Auschwitz. Bericht über die Strafsache gegen Mulka u.a. vor dem Schwurgericht Frankfurt*, Frankfurt am Main, 1968

Orth, Karin, *Das System der nationalsozialistischen Konzentrationslager. Eine politische Organisationgeschichte*, Hamburg, 1999

Pelt, Robert Jan van, *The Case for Auschwitz. Evidence from the Irving Trial*, Bloomington, Indiana, 2002

Piper, Franciszek, *Die Zahl der Opfer von Auschwitz. Aufgrund der Quellen und der Erträge der Forschung, 1945 bis 1990*, Oświęcim, 1993 (originally published in Polish, 1992)

Pohl, Dieter, *Holocaust. Die Ursachen, das Geschehen, die Folgen*, Freiburg im Breisgau, 2000

Pressac, Jean-Claude, *Die Krematorien von Auschwitz. Die Technik des Massenmords*, Munich, 1995 (originally published in French, 1993)

Schulte, Jan-Erik, *Zwangsarbeit und Vernichtung: Das Wirtschaftsimperium der SS. Oswald Pohl und das SS-Wirtschaftsverwaltungshauptampt 1933–1945*, Paderborn, 2001

Steinbacher, Sybille, *'Musterstadt' Auschwitz. Germanisierungspolitik und Judenmord in Ostoberschlesien*, Munich, 2000

Strzelecki, Andrzej, *The Evacuation, Dismantling and Liberation of KL Auschwitz*, Oświęcim, 2001 (originally published in Polish, 1982)

Wagner, Bernd C., *IG Auschwitz. Zwangsarbeit und Vernichtung von Häftlingen des Lagers Monowitz 1941–1945*, Munich, 2000

Werle, Gerhard and Thomas Wandres, *Auschwitz vor Gericht. Völkermord und bundesdeutsche Strafjustiz*, Munich, 1995

Wojak, Irmtrud (ed.), *Auschwitz-Prozess 4 Ks/63 Frankfurt am Main*, Cologne, 2004

Wojak, Irmtrud (ed.), *'Gerichtstag halten über uns selbst . . .' Geschichte und Wirkungsgeschichte des ersten*

Frankfurter Auschwitz-Prozesses. Jahrbuch des Fritz-Bauer-Instituts, Frankfurt am Main, 2001

Yahil, Leni, *The Holocaust: The Fate of European Jewry, 1932–1945*, Oxford, 1990 (originally published in Hebrew, 1987)

Zimmermann, Michael, *Rassenutopie und Genozid. Die nationalsozialistische 'Lösung der Zigeunerfrage'*, Hamburg, 1996

Index of names

Index of names